THE
Missing PIECE

BY RHYS THOMAS

Getting Clear About Your
Soul's Purpose for Success in Life

DEDICATION

To my students who have all become my teachers.

What people are saying

> *"I use the Rhys Method Life Purpose Profiles® with my high end clients because it is an incredibly powerful personal growth tool. It quickly helps me and my staff assess our clients' deeper mission in life to help them build business and life strategies based on their Profile. The Profiles make it crystal clear how certain people self sabotage and how to redirect their negative patterns and get them back standing in their power again."*

MARGARET M. LYNCH
SUCCESS COACHING, MargaretMLynch.com

Getting Clear About Your Soul's Purpose for Success in Life

"Before discovering the Rhys Method Life Purpose Profiles®, I had already spent many years trying to understand myself and others better. I was familiar with the Enneagram, astrology, Ayurvedic doshas, Chinese medicine elements. All of these frameworks had gifts and taught me something about myself and what I was here to do, but none of them answered the whole question.

Then I came across Rhys' program, and I was blown away. I kept wanting more, and more, and more…it is the most thorough, simple, and consistent way of understanding myself and others that I have ever come across. As Rhys teaches, my purpose isn't something I am going to do, it is someone I am going to be. Different than some of the other systems I've used, the Life Purpose Profiles are universal, and I can relate to all five of them both within myself and in others.

As I start to settle more into who I am, life is a lot more fun, things flow better, I worry a lot less, and I'm now going about creating my business from the inside out instead of the other way around. Plus, I feel like a magician when I work with clients or even relate to friends and am able to 'see' them in a powerful and profound way due to looking at them through the lens of the Profiles. And my most important relationship—the one I have with myself—has dramatically changed, therefore shifting all the other relationships in my life. There is still so much more to learn, but I could stop now and the Profiles would have forever changed my life."

MARTHA HANSON

CONTENTS

www.RhysMethod.com | www.RhysThomasInstitute.com

ACKNOWLEDGEMENTS

This book is made possible by all of you who have contributed to me and my work over the years. I could never have written it without the gifts each of you brought to me from your unique soul's perspective. My deepest gratitude goes out to you all.

In particular, I want to acknowledge:
My family for their support and patience while I spent long hours doing research in my study, and especially to Trevyr and Logan, my sons, who listened generously to my "crazy ideas."

My teachers, some of whom I've never met, who inspired me: Alexander Lowen, Eva Pierrakos, Dorothy Martin Neville, Wayne Dyer, Deepak Chopra, Eckhart Tolle, and Martin Luther King, Jr.

My team of editors and artists: Nancy Marriott at New Paradigm Writing and Editing Services, Rachel Dunham at Brand Therapy, and Shann Vander Leek at True Balance International, for their tireless efforts in helping me put my ideas into words and pictures to produce a book that could communicate my teachings.

My students, too numerous to mention but who have been part of my living laboratory as I developed my ideas into practices. Especially, all those students who now work alongside me as teachers and administrators at the Institute to support others to find their life purpose and live an extraordinary life.

PREFACE

There is an epidemic in the world today that no one sees. You can't see it, but you can feel it, sometimes in the pit of your stomach or when you wake up in the middle of the night, asking, *Is this all there is?*

I'm referring to the sweeping sense we all have just below the surface that the life we are living is without purpose, without meaning, without the deep satisfaction and fulfillment we were meant to have, we deserve to have.

It is the missing piece.

No matter how successful you may be in your career and finances or in your intimate and business relationships, it's still there, that undeniable feeling that something big is missing, something important that would make a difference in your life.

You might be feeling the emptiness when you are heading off to work or getting up to take care of your children, day in and day out. Or you feel it at day's end when the gap between what you had hoped to accomplish and what you actually did accomplish leave you rundown or frustrated. The struggle, the overwhelm, the sacrifice, the self-sabotage—all of these experiences are pointing at what is missing in your life, which I believe is this: you knowing beyond a doubt what your purpose is, and having the courage and energy to pursue it.

For the past 15 years, I've been helping people to find their missing piece so they can have what they really want in their life. As founder of the Rhys Thomas Institute of Energy Healing, I've polled thousands of my clients and students, and found that most people want three very basic things: financial freedom and career they are proud of, better relationships both personally and in business, and better health so they can have a lifetime of fun in the career they love and with all the people they know.

This book is about how you can get those basic things we all want in life. In the following chapters, you will be shown the concrete tools you need to know your life purpose and get back the joy in life you know you deserve. The three easy steps I teach you for getting what you want in life are so simple, you probably are already aware of them. First, you need to acquire clarity of purpose and direction that is more than what you were told you *should* be doing, but rather is your calling in life. Second, you let that calling give you the courage to step toward it and act fearlessly. And lastly, you find the energy to do it every day until you break your procrastination habits and start living in all areas of your life motivated by a deep sense of mission.

As you may have guessed, the most important part of this path is not only knowing who you are and what your life purpose is, but also knowing when you are chasing a dream or a have gone off track due to what you *think* is your purpose. Once you use these tools as a way to attain inner direction, fearless courage, and limitless energy for yourself, you will be able to find much broader success in all the other relationships in your life.

There is a simple maxim: If you know how to get other people what they really want in life, you will be rewarded beyond what you have ever imagined. The system that you will learn to help you do that is the Rhys Method Life Purpose Profile System®, and you may find it to be the most important set of skills you ever acquire. As you cultivate your skill, you become someone who can motivate and inspire others, not just in your own language but in theirs as well. I am sure if you are reading these pages you would love to own the market in your business, or be the spouse and parent of the year to your family. With my system, that is entirely possible.

What this book won't give you is a gimmick or trick for finding the missing piece you've been looking for. Neither will there be any impossible-to-understand self assessment systems that leave you feeling like a number or an astrological sign that you need a PhD to apply in your life. You will be able to easily understand and apply this information to your life the day you read it—it's about who you are and everyone else truly is.

Is this something you want? Whether the system of self-awareness on these pages is what you want to transform you or not depends on how fed up you are with pushing that rock up the hill every day called "my life" and not even knowing if it is actually your real life! Or, you may have a fairly good idea

Getting Clear About Your Soul's Purpose for Success in Life

of who you are but have no idea how to motivate your children or your staff. You may have certain clients that you lose because you just can't get them what they want. Or you are great at getting things to happen in your life and business but have a terrible habit of sabotaging yourself before you actually get the benefits.

You need to be prepared to let go of the illusion of who you think you are or who you think you are supposed to be—if you are going to truly discover your deeper purpose. You will also need to let go of the illusion you have of who other people are and realize how seeing them through the limiting filter you have is what is causing the problems. If you are not ready for that and would prefer to just think about the changes you know you have to make, this book and its tools may not be what you are looking for.

I have worked with thousands of people who are very much like you, heart-centered and successful people who have already studied many systems and looked under many rocks to find their true calling but still find something is missing. Like they once did, you are probably wondering if there is more to life. I have been sharing the "more" with clients and students through my work and seminars and in the Rhys Thomas Institute of Energy Medicine over the last 15 years. The huge success and rapid expansion of my school has been fueled directly by the use of the Rhys Method Life Purpose Profile System® you are about to learn in this book. The transformation that has happened for thousands can and will happen for you.

When people discover their deepest sense of purpose, it is truly remarkable. Success in marriages, businesses, and family relationships are not only common but the norm. And successful people innately know how to inspire, motivate, and influence other people, giving them more courage and more energy, and helping them to break limiting patterns and beliefs to succeed in whatever do. The Rhys Method Life Purpose Profile System® will take you beyond the best of the best motivators, business owners, parents, teachers, and coaches. It gives you an amazing transformational tool that will make you an indispensible resource in whatever field you are in.

If you are ready to find the missing piece in your life, turn the page and let's get started. It's time to stop talking about living and start doing it.

INTRODUCING THE
Rhys Method Life Purpose Profile System®

Meet the 5 Kinds of People
in the World…

…to discover who you are
and how knowing each of them
can help you get what you want in life.

There is an ancient Hindu proverb that says, *The Three Great Mysteries are: air to a bird, water to a fish, mankind to himself.* We are going to take mankind off that list. It all starts with you looking deeper into the people you already know and seeing yourself in them.

At the beginning of each chapter that follows, I will share with you about my five favorite people in the world and their unique missions. You will see yourself in some of them, and in others you will see people you know in your life.

FLALT

Each of my friends represents a particular profile of qualities that come from within them—their unique Life Purpose Profile. All together, these are the five kinds of people in the world, based on their energetic, soul-sourced blueprint. They are the *thinkers*, the *feelers*, the *caretakers*, the *achievers*, and the *leaders* of the world, each one a unique blend of all the qualities, while being strongest in one or two.

In the chapter that follows after you meet each one, you will get a more detailed description of the unique Life Purpose Profile they represent, along with some other features that support you to know yourself better and people in your life just like them.

Keep in mind as you meet my friends that I'm referring to real people, even though I've changed their names for reasons of privacy. Some are women, some are men, but the qualities and defenses each one expresses are universal in that neither gender has any claim to them. As you read, you may recognize yourself or an important person in your life of the opposite gender of my friend.

But here's what is most important about you getting to know these five kinds of people: They are your greatest resource for having the life you want, because knowing people like them and how you can help those people get what *they* want is the key to your own success.

Use your new found clarity to become inspired and motivated in your own life and also to inspire and motivate others— whether spouse, children, friends, or when working with clients and students professionally. The Rhys Method

Life Purpose Profile System® allows you to see into the depths of the soul, unleashing your ability to create the life you desire and empower others to do the same.

MEET MY FRIEND MARK…

I'd like you to meet one of my favorite people in life, my friend Mark.

You may know someone just like Mark in your own life. As you read, ask yourself if he doesn't remind you of a son, father, child, teacher, spouse—or anyone in any role or relationship in your life. Maybe even *you*!

I share a lot in common with Mark, so much so that it's hard to admit I am so like him at times. But while I see myself in him, I can also honor my friend for his unique qualities and how perfectly he expresses them in the world.

Mark is intelligent, thoughtful, highly creative and artistic. Even though he is not a young man, he can be extremely playful and innocent at times, making time spent with him seem like a fun game. Mark has chosen to apply his brilliance to science, but he is equally well versed in spirituality, religion, art, philosophy, politics, fencing, chess, conspiracy theory, and the latest jokes flying around the Internet.

Maybe someone you know is as brilliant and creative as Mark, someone who has a mind like Einstein, constantly alert and inquiring. I'm not talking about the analytical kind of mind, but rather the mind that is always asking about the true meaning of life, never satisfied with a superficial version.

Mark is a musician with a profound understanding of how sound and light can be used to awaken the body and mind. He is often lost in thought about how the universe is influencing the neo-political agenda, or just trying to remember what he had for breakfast. Maybe someone you know can expound on universal principles but forgets to eat. People like Mark seem to inhabit a world that most of us don't even see, but if you ask them, they're always happy to share that world with you. Keeping up with their brilliance, however, can make you regret you ever asked!

Did you ever have a professor like Mark? Did you have a silly friend in high school that would lie out on the grass summer nights and stare at the stars with you, questioning what might hold them all up there? Think about yourself a moment. Do you have a tendency, like Mark, to live in higher realms of thought and spirit?

As amazing and brilliant as Mark is, on his bad days he has so much anxiety that he wants to hide from the world. You'll often find him in safe place away from the punishing unconsciousness and aggression of people—the lab, the New Age book store, or even wandering about in the woods. He and people like him can and do become dissociated from life when they live in their fear, tending to spend much of their time in their heads, spinning with ideas that never seem to land productively. If you tend to neglect feelings in your body and go off on mental excursions that can last for days or months, you may be like Mark.

In the *Rhys Method Life Purpose Profile System®*, we give a name to the kind of person Mark is, and even though a name can't truly capture the essence of a person, we all know people like Mark. By giving them a name, we honor these people's deepest soul qualities; in Mark's case that name is the Creative Idealist. On a bad day, when life is just too scary for the *Creative Idealist* to be present and in their bodies, we say that people like Mark are in *Thinker* defense.

Enjoy the Creative Idealists in your life. Listen to them, for they are talking about what is truly possible for you and for all of humanity. To learn more about them, and how you can support them, coach them, live with them and love them, read on for an in-depth description. You will also learn how to embrace these soul quality gifts within yourself and become aware of the devastating defensive behaviors that occur when we forget the truth of who we are.

PROFILE I

THE CREATIVE IDEALIST

with Thinker Defense

PROFILE DESCRIPTION

The Creative Idealist Profile, in both light (balanced) and dark (defended) aspects is described below. You will see how the *core soul quality* of this Profile flows freely outward into the world or is distorted into a false self called the Profile's *defense*.

Your core soul quality is your individual essence, the eternal part of you that was there the day you were born and never changes. As your primary life energy, it radiates out from your center through six levels: feeling/sensation, emotional, action, mental, worldly, and spiritual.

But when that same energy of your core soul quality is diverted into your defense, you live life from a limited perspective and have no real power. Each of the five Life Purpose Profiles you will learn about reacts and goes into defense uniquely. Your defense is not who you are; rather it is the way you react when you have forgotten who you really are. Your path back to wholeness and balance, your natural state, is available through first identifying and then living in your own Life Purpose Profile.

CREATIVE IDEALISTS YOU MAY KNOW *include the playful and highly creative artist in their core but who in defense stay holed up in their studio ignoring their wife and kids; the spiritual teacher who can plumb the secrets of the universe but in defense sounds a little off his rocker when he starts to talk about his views; the client who has an enormous vision for benefiting humankind, but in defense can't seem to write that first book chapter or get the simplest project off the ground.*

IN THEIR **CORE SOUL QUALITY**, Creative Idealists are intellectual and artistic pioneers and thinkers who do not see the world the same as other people do. They know themselves through being a creative force that constantly brings newness to the world. They are fun, playful, comedic and sometimes a bit nutty. They love to play with ideas and are often irreverent. They feel their soul's deep connection to a source of wisdom beyond the Earth plane and channel it to bring new ideas to the world.

Getting Clear About Your Soul's Purpose for Success in Life

In defense, *Thinkers* deal in mental concepts only and live in a constant state of feeling as if they don't really exist or have a purpose. They rarely come into their bodies for full expression. Their soul is not a point of reference but a world they live in off the planet that is not interested in the struggles of a human life. They do know they have a soul but only in the spirit world, not here on Earth.

AT THE FEELING LEVEL, Creative Idealists are super sensitive to higher frequencies and feel higher guidance and spirit with all of their senses. They are in tune with spiritual knowing and awareness directly, and don't know how they know what they know. They have the ability to sense brilliant ideas and visions coming forward and can channel them directly from their connection to their soul.

In defense, *Thinkers* are in a constant state of fear, blocking all other sensations. If you ask them how they are feeling, they reply in language that expresses fear and uncertainty. They don't have a range of feeling, only a range of fear and anxiety. They do not honor feelings in themselves or others because feelings are simply mental activities.

AT THE EMOTIONAL LEVEL, Creative Idealists are enthusiastic about diversity and the infinite possibility of life's expression. They laugh and express humor freely. They are able to experience the deepest spiritual states of universal love, oneness, and spiritual ecstasy, but they struggle with basic human emotions that are more complex.

In defense, *Thinkers'* emotions are fear-based and hyper-focused on avoiding any aggression or confrontation. Any emotion that makes them more present and engaged with the world, and therefore more vulnerable, must be avoided. There is no passion expressed in bringing ideas to the world; they prefer to hide emotionally in order to feel safe.

AT THE ACTION LEVEL, Creative Idealists juggle many balls at once, rarely having just one job or hobby, which would be too boring for them. Creative Idealists are creation machines, letting their flow of consciousness lead them constantly on, always tweaking and improving on yesterday's ideas. One brilliant project leads to another in a never-ending stream.

In defense, *Thinkers* rarely leave the mental realm to act productively and can be doing many things but always in a scattered way. They are the seekers who never want to find what they are seeking. They unconsciously sabotage getting anything done because if they actually did put a stake in the ground, someone could squash it or steal it, so they keep moving.

AT THE MENTAL LEVEL, Creative Idealists have incredibly dynamic minds, always mentally on, always creative. They are never at a loss for something new and exciting to say. Unlike most who may use thinking as a means to get somewhere, Creative Idealists enjoy thinking for the pure pleasure of it. They channel a level of consciousness that is beyond worldly, and it is through that connection that they know their highest calling in life.

In defense, *Thinkers* prefer theory to real life. They rarely check in with reality, but prefer to imagine a reality that is uniquely their own. They can be total space shots or hardcore scientists for whom life is just a test tube experiment, not real in any way.

AT THE WORLDLY LEVEL, Creative Idealists love to create newness in and for the world, bringing their brilliant ideas forward to benefit all. They create artwork that lasts a lifetime, and everyone who sees it is awakened to deeper ideas they share. They create ever new channels on the Internet for faster and more amazing ways of connecting individual minds to one another.

In defense, *Thinkers* are disconnected from the world and community. Their brilliant ideas rarely evolve into products or services that benefit others but remain hidden in notebooks and on computers, never to be seen out of their fear of being attacked for their ideas and radical notions. They are dissociated from life and will be the computer hackers, fighting the world in invisible ways.

AT THE SPIRITUAL LEVEL, People who embody the Creative Idealist understand universal principles and see them in everything and everyone. They have an incredible connection to their inner brilliance and easily perceive divinity in all things. They see clearly how spirit is embodying itself through all things, and they create from that flow of life force, not from any static mental process.

In defense, *Thinkers* have their head in the stars, lost in a world of extraneous realities. They can be found haunting New Age bookstore around the world, hiding in ashrams, meditation groups, Buddhist monasteries, studying Zen, Scientology, astrology, quantum physics, *The Secret*, and on and on. But none of it ever leads to true change, being only a way to avoid life and not be present for it. They use spirituality as an escape, never something that grounds them in any way.

BULL'S EYE PROFILE CHARTS

As you look at the Bull's Eye Charts that follow for each of the five Profiles, notice how in the balanced system, the core soul quality at the center radiates out freely and unblocked from one level to the next and ultimately reaches out through the entire universe. A balanced system is dynamic and resilient. It naturally has all the energy and courage needed for you to make tough life choices and meet the challenges that lead to fulfilling your unique life purpose—even when others might not approve.

In the out-of-balance system Bull's Eye Chart, the core soul quality is either *deficient or excessive* at a particular level. A person will reflect a deficiency when they avoid or procrastinate at that level of their life, or become excessive when they try to solve problems at that level by only one behavior, leaving them stuck in repetitive and self-sabotaging patterns. Each person goes into defense uniquely, according to their Profile. Knowing how and when you go into defense gives you the ability to find your way back toward balance and guide others to do the same.

When that primal energy of *who you truly are* is free from defense, balanced and unblocked, your natural ability to create whatever you *really* want in life is unleashed and you become unstoppable in all that you do.

THE CREATIVE IDEALIST BALANCED SYSTEM
BULL'S EYE CHART

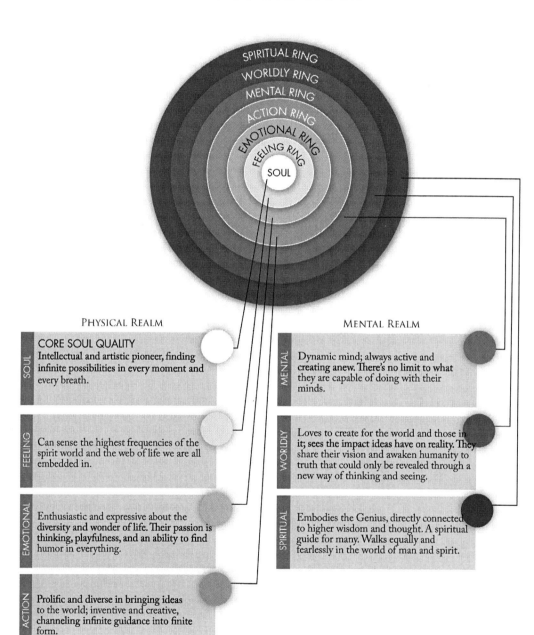

PHYSICAL REALM

CORE SOUL QUALITY
SOUL — Intellectual and artistic pioneer, finding infinite possibilities in every moment and every breath.

FEELING — Can sense the highest frequencies of the spirit world and the web of life we are all embedded in.

EMOTIONAL — Enthusiastic and expressive about the diversity and wonder of life. Their passion is thinking, playfulness, and an ability to find humor in everything.

ACTION — Prolific and diverse in bringing ideas to the world; inventive and creative, channeling infinite guidance into finite form.

MENTAL REALM

MENTAL — Dynamic mind; always active and creating anew. There's no limit to what they are capable of doing with their minds.

WORLDLY — Loves to create for the world and those in it; sees the impact ideas have on reality. They share their vision and awaken humanity to truth that could only be revealed through a new way of thinking and seeing.

SPIRITUAL — Embodies the Genius, directly connected to higher wisdom and thought. A spiritual guide for many. Walks equally and fearlessly in the world of man and spirit.

Getting Clear About Your Soul's Purpose for Success in Life

THE THINKER OUT OF BALANCE
BULL'S EYE CHART

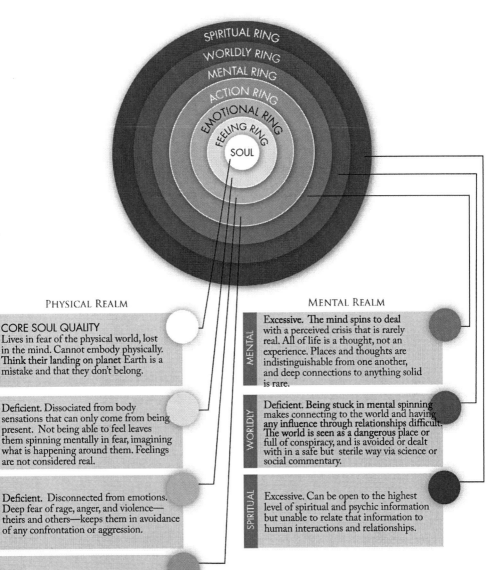

PHYSICAL REALM

CORE SOUL QUALITY
Lives in fear of the physical world, lost in the mind. Cannot embody physically. Think their landing on planet Earth is a mistake and that they don't belong.

Deficient. Dissociated from body sensations that can only come from being present. Not being able to feel leaves them spinning mentally in fear, imagining what is happening around them. Feelings are not considered real.

Deficient. Disconnected from emotions. Deep fear of rage, anger, and violence—theirs and others—keeps them in avoidance of any confrontation or aggression.

Deficient. Actions occur only in intellectual pursuits and tend to be scattered, not connected to everyday reality.

MENTAL REALM

Excessive. The mind spins to deal with a perceived crisis that is rarely real. All of life is a thought, not an experience. Places and thoughts are indistinguishable from one another, and deep connections to anything solid is rare.

Deficient. Being stuck in mental spinning makes connecting to the world and having any influence through relationships difficult. The world is seen as a dangerous place or full of conspiracy, and is avoided or dealt with in a safe but sterile way via science or social commentary.

Excessive. Can be open to the highest level of spiritual and psychic information but unable to relate that information to human interactions and relationships.

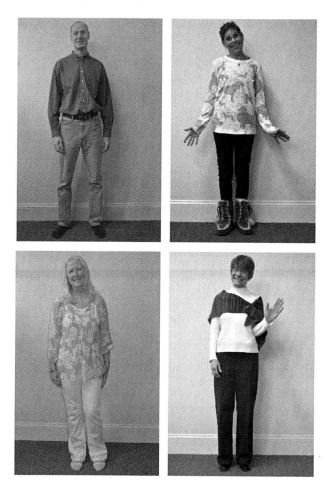

When you are visually assessing a person's Profile, notice that the Creative Idealist/Thinker either has a nervous energy or appears slightly vacant, lost in thought even when having their picture taken. Creative Idealists are usually very thin, with a vertically moving energy, and can be very tall; the man shown in the upper left is 6'5". You will often see a head tilt, indicating how the mind and body are disconnected and frequently in different worlds. The Creative Idealist's most salient traits are being funny, silly and witty. They are sensitive and gentle souls who would rather flee than stand and fight when confronted by any conflict.

CELEBRITY/MEDIA EXAMPLES

JIM HENSON

KALEY CUOCO

ALBERT EINSTEIN

GOLDIE HAWN

HOW TO EMPOWER PEOPLE IN THE THINKER DEFENSE

Being able to motivate someone who is stuck in self-sabotaging behaviors and attitudes is not easy, but it is so much easier when you know who you are dealing with and how they may sabotage themselves from being in defense. Creative Idealist in Thinker Defense sabotage themselves through fear and anxiety, getting lost in mental spinning and being unable to make decisions.

Think of your clients, your family members, your friends and coworkers who might fit this Profile. You can help them to get out of defense and back to their balanced and resourceful state, their core soul self. Only when connected to their soul will they have what they want in life, not what their limited, defended self is providing.

Here are some ways to empower the Thinkers in your life:
1. Never tell them to get organized or grounded.
2. Be irreverent and make their crazy, ironic thinking fun and important.
3. Accept their non-presence and teach them how they are present.
4. Never be aggressive with them physically or emotionally. Keep conversation and emotions light and more intellectual until they are out of defense, then use soft, safe emotions.

YOUR PERSONAL *Life Purpose Profile* WORKSHEET

Here is a chance for you to apply what you've learned. Answer the questions below to sharpen your vision of your own life's purpose and then be able to help others to do the same. Knowing your direction and mission is the key to having what you really want in life, today not tomorrow!

1. Do you see yourself in the description of this Profile, either in balance or in defense?

    ○ YES!   ○ SOMEWHAT   ○ VERY LITTLE

> *(If you answered **Very Little**, then you want to read about the other four Profiles to find if another description fits better for you. Skip question #2 for now and answer question #4 on this worksheet about other people in your life.)*

2. If you answered *Yes* or *Somewhat* above, take a moment and write down how your Creative Idealist core quality supports you in your career, relationships and health. Then write how being in your Thinker defense sabotages you in those same areas.

CREATIVE IDEALIST CORE SOUL QUALITY:

Career/Financial Freedom _____

Relationship Fulfillment _____

Vibrant Health and Well-being _____

THINKER DEFENSE:

Career/Financial Freedom _____

Relationship Fulfillment _____

Vibrant Health and Well-being _____

3. Now write some steps you could take that would support you to live more in your core soul quality:

1 _____

2 _____

3 _____

4. Do you recognize people in your life that fit the qualities of this Profile, both balanced and in defense? If so, choose one specific person and write about **A)** the impact he or she has had on your life, and **B)** how you might best relate to that person to support them when they are in defense to be restored to balance.

A _____

B _____

MEET MY FRIEND LYNDA…

I want to introduce you to another one of my favorite people in life, Lynda.

You may know someone just like Lynda, and as you read about her, ask yourself who she reminds you of—a sister, a lover, a friend, a mother or daughter? Maybe you'll find she reminds you of yourself.

Lynda is someone I would have avoided or judged harshly years ago, when I used to think the best way to go through life was to have a thick-skin and hold it all together. Now I realize that Lynda and people like her are the ones who melt the hard hearts of people like me and show us what is really important in life.

There is a softness about Lynda. She is beautiful, radiant, and loving. She has never raised a finger to hurt another soul or creature, and never could. She has a gentle voice that may get drowned out by the din of daily life, but when she looks at me and speaks, it is the emotion in her voice and eyes that remind me real love does exist, regardless of all the wars and devastation going on in the world.

Do you know someone as soft and loving as Lynda, with an embrace that is as accepting as Mother Mary, has a keen aesthetic sense for beauty, and who always takes your side whenever you are wronged? Maybe she was your favorite aunt growing up or a teacher in grade school who always came to your rescue when you needed help.

Lynda dresses to feel good, rarely wearing brand names or professional clothing but rather garments that create a fluid appearance as she walks gently through the world. Her style is simple and elegant. She seems to resist nothing, loving it all—or at least gracefully accepting even the greatest challenges life may throw her way.

She moves from loving her pets, to loving small children, to loving the adults who search her out because of the way she touches their hearts and makes them feel like a child again—always open to love. This might be the person in your life who forgives you no matter how bad you act, or will cajole you out of a bad mood when you've had a long day and are frustrated with your boss or co-workers.

Surprisingly, Lynda feels that the love she has to offer is never enough, knowing that the world values things and objects, and what she brings to life cannot be measured. But Lynda's gifts have their true value in the place where it counts—the heart and soul—and so they often go underappreciated.

Lynda can be needy and helpless at times, overwhelmed by the sheer brutality and fast pace of living on planet Earth. She often must take the time to retreat to some quiet place of contemplation and nature to heal and restore herself. This may be what you need at times, when you feel bruised by other people's insensitivity or hurt by love not returned.

If you're like Lynda, you might have noticed that well-meaning do-gooders try to fix you and get you to toughen up, so you can bring more of your gifts out into the world. But my friend Lynda actually enjoys crying at sad movies and being moved by those heart-tugging TV commercials, and when others laugh, she is more likely to cry with joy. She's not afraid to have her heart broken five times a day, because she knows that a broken heart is an open heart, one that can fall in love over and over again.

If you know someone who may be like my friend Lynda, and you are trying to fix that person or get them to toughen up, don't. Possibly that quality of vulnerability and emotional freedom they embody reminds you that you, too, have a broken, open heart. The power you mistake for weakness in Lynda may just be the power that will teach everyone to love with an open heart and eventually change the planet for the better.

We honor the kind of person Lynda is in the *Rhys Method Life Purpose Profile System®* by giving them the title *Emotional Intelligence Specialist*. These are the soft, gentle, and emotional people you know, the ones whose sensitivity to beauty and often child-like innocence indicate their heart of unconditional love. On a bad day, when the Emotional Intelligence Specialist is not expressing their deepest soul qualities, but retreating in self-pity and hopelessness because life is just too overwhelming, we call them the *Poor Me* in defense.

Enjoy the soft and gentle people in your life, and tell them you love them just the way they are. To learn more about them, and how you can support them, coach them, live with them and love them, read on for an in-depth description. You will also learn how to embrace these soul quality gifts within yourself and become aware of the devastating defensive behaviors that occur when we forget the truth of who we are.

THE EMOTIONAL INTELLIGENCE SPECIALIST

with Poor Me Defense

Getting Clear About Your Soul's Purpose for Success in Life

PROFILE DESCRIPTION

The Emotional Intelligence Specialist Profile, in both light (balanced) and dark (defended) aspects is described below. You will see how the *core soul quality* of this Profile flows freely outward into the world or is distorted into a false self called the Profile's *defense*.

Your core soul quality is your individual essence, the eternal part of you that was there the day you were born and never changes. As your primary life energy, it radiates out from your center through six levels: feeling/sensation, emotional, action, mental, worldly, and spiritual.

But when that same energy of your core soul quality is diverted into your defense, you live life from a limited perspective and have no real power. Each of the five Life Purpose Profiles you will learn about reacts and goes into defense uniquely. Your defense is not who you are; rather it is the way you react when you have forgotten who you really are. Your path back to wholeness and balance, your natural state, is available through first identifying and then living in your own Life Purpose Profile.

EMOTIONAL INTELLIGENCE SPECIALISTS YOU MAY KNOW *are the friend or relative who in her core is always surrounded by exquisite beauty in her home, her clothing, and her work environment but in defense has to order everything from catalogues because she can't stand to shop in crowds. She's the girlfriend or wife who is moved to tears at the least mention of harming an animal or child, or the daughter or son who can't stand up to the tougher kids in school and collapses when confronted for the slightest error.*

IN THEIR **CORE SOUL QUALITY**, Emotional Intelligence Specialists are lovers, constantly nurturing the world and those in it through unconditional love and understanding. They are love in their very core and at the soul level positively exude that love.

In defense, *Poor Mes* are aware they have an authentic self but can't differentiate it from that of others. This keeps them from radiating that soul level love and being present with others in their unique authentic self.

AT THE FEELING LEVEL, Emotional Intelligence Specialists are incredibly sensitive and psychically attuned to the feelings of self and others. When they are balanced, they can sense another having a feeling and don't mistake it as their own; at the same time, they have compassion for the other as they are having that feeling. They can recognize the difference between themselves and another when it comes to senses and feelings they might be experiencing. They can also sense that the way they feel life is uniquely theirs, and they are never in resistance to the sensations in life, even negative ones.

In defense, *Poor Mes* are very sensitive to subtle energies, with no healthy boundaries for protection, and so are very vulnerable and needy. Often, they can't tell the difference between their own feelings and the feelings of others; they think they are having feelings that belong to other people, but they're only projecting their own feelings on to others. For example, Poor Me mothers identify their child's feelings as being the same as their own and assume they are always feeling the same things together.

AT THE EMOTIONAL LEVEL, Emotional Intelligence Specialists have a rich emotional life, experiencing and expressing much love and joy. They feel the whole expanse of life and aren't afraid of their emotions because an emotion only exists in this present moment, and they only live in the present moment. They often don't know what time it is because now is the only thing that counts. They are fearless in their ability to hold and transmute complex emotions that drive others to distraction.

In defense, *Poor Mes* magnify their feelings to experience excessive emotional mood swings. They can never seem to get enough and will often have addictive personalities. They have strong needs to connect emotionally, be deeply loved, be held, but when these needs are not met, secondary pleasures such as people, drugs, alcohol, food, and sex may be used to fill that hole.

AT THE ACTION LEVEL, Emotional Intelligence Specialists are sensitive teachers and their sweet, loving, supportive actions help others understand their own feelings. They are often Kindergarten teachers, working with young children to help them with their emotions in an educational system that mostly denies emotions. Everything they do is the embodiment of love.

In defense, *Poor Mes* spend all their energy on expressing emotions, leaving nothing for taking effective action. When they do, it's too little, too late. They can't fight their own battles, because they are too soft and eventually just collapse when in conflict.

AT THE MENTAL LEVEL, Emotional Intelligence Specialists have brilliant emotional intelligence of self and others, and are able to help anyone with the complicated emotions in life, such as grief. They are able to handle hundreds of subtle emotional capacities that humans have just by living their lives and recognizing the infinite complexity of human emotions. They have gentle caring thoughts and help those who are highly critical of themselves find a new way of seeing themselves.

In defense, the *Poor Me* is excessive, overly focused on their own emotional wounding, and constantly talking about it. They tend to speak in an emotional language, such as, *How'd you feel about that? Let me tell you about how I felt about that.* They think constantly about how they were rejected emotionally, and about how they shouldn't be having so much emotion, telling themselves, *I'm so overwhelmed… It's so exhausting.*

AT THE WORLDLY LEVEL, Emotional Intelligence Specialists support people in their world one at a time. When they get in a group of adults, they have a difficult time holding their energy field because they want to connect deeply to only one at a time. When they are interacting with children, the children hold a group consciousness that they can easily be in relationship with, and at the same time are able to see each child as separate.

In defense, *Poor Mes* become easily overwhelmed by the world. They don't usually experience depression, but when they do, they don't have enough energy to stay in it. They may feel broken, but then are okay, then broken again and okay again, flowing quickly from one state to the other. Poor Mes only get stuck when they resist their feelings, holding them back after being told they are "too emotional." Instead of being depressed, they become victims and try to disappear, saying and thinking, *I can't even be who I am—poor me!*

AT THE SPIRITUAL LEVEL, Emotional Intelligence Specialists embody the Mother Mary energy of unconditional love for all beings, making them among the most powerful beings on the planet. They don't engage in wars, build corporations, or do anything other than making sure every person they meet knows they are loved, one at a time. Each person whose heart is awakened, can then share that with others.

Emotional Intelligence Specialists know that is their mission and don't listen to the voice that says, *You gotta toughen up and get out there and start working. Be more disciplined!* They may try that on for a period of time and finally realize it's not their purpose. Their purpose is to be soft, loving, and help people become conscious through their feelings. Emotional Intelligence Specialists are our greatest hope in people learning the connection of consciousness to feeling.

In defense, *Poor Mes* are conditioned to believe, as we all are, that love is something given only to us by others, not coming from within ourselves. For Emotional Intelligences Specialists, this is devastating because it negates the one thing they are made of, their very essence, which is love. They are wired to just be love, and yet they're taught as children that love comes from other people. This makes them always dependent and needy of others in relationship for love and attention, having no access to the source from within themselves. They feel empty and abandoned by people whom they want to love them most, even when those people do actually love them.

THE EMOTIONAL INTELLIGENCE SPECIALIST
BALANCED SYSTEM
BULL'S EYE CHART

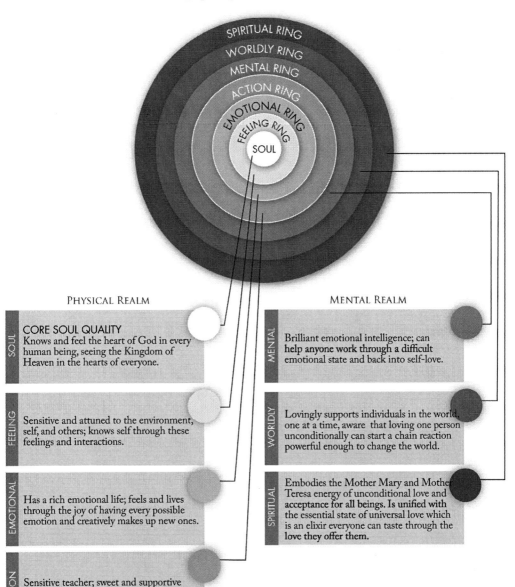

SPIRITUAL RING
WORLDLY RING
MENTAL RING
ACTION RING
EMOTIONAL RING
FEELING RING
SOUL

PHYSICAL REALM

SOUL
CORE SOUL QUALITY
Knows and feel the heart of God in every human being, seeing the Kingdom of Heaven in the hearts of everyone.

FEELING
Sensitive and attuned to the environment, self, and others; knows self through these feelings and interactions.

EMOTIONAL
Has a rich emotional life; feels and lives through the joy of having every possible emotion and creatively makes up new ones.

ACTION
Sensitive teacher; sweet and supportive in every action for self and others. Actions are gentle and reverent.

MENTAL REALM

MENTAL
Brilliant emotional intelligence; can help anyone work through a difficult emotional state and back into self-love.

WORLDLY
Lovingly supports individuals in the world, one at a time, aware that loving one person unconditionally can start a chain reaction powerful enough to change the world.

SPIRITUAL
Embodies the Mother Mary and Mother Teresa energy of unconditional love and acceptance for all beings. Is unified with the essential state of universal love which is an elixir everyone can taste through the love they offer them.

THE POOR ME OUT OF BALANCE
BULL'S EYE CHART

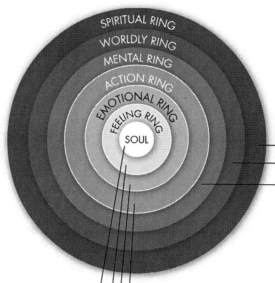

PHYSICAL REALM

SOUL

CORE SOUL QUALITY
Open. Is aware of their soul, but that awareness triggers a longing for the unified state that is limited in human form. They fixate on merging with others rather than feeling their own soul as full of love.

FEELING

Excessive. They have no filter, so all of life comes in uninvited, and they are at the mercy of the energies around them. This leads to constant flooding energetically and not being in tune with the subtle guidance of sensations and feelings.

EMOTIONAL

Excessive. May explode in hysteria or implode with depression or addictive neediness, and every emotion in between. The raw energy of the soul gets dissipated at this level before it is grounded in action. With no model for how to handle the flood of their own emotions, they project outward and blame others for how they feel.

ACTION

Deficient. Emotional energy is spent trying to get others to fill their needs, so they are exhausted by emotions, not energized. Little energy remains for the inner discipline needed to take action on life issues.

MENTAL REALM

MENTAL

Excessive. Instead of acting, they talk and process feelings and needs, often going in circles and fixating on their feelings, which easily get stuck in the negative. Mental energy is spent on talking about or around problems, or feeling justified in having them.

WORLDLY

Deficient. Demands that the other person or the world be responsible for their emotional well-being in a child-like way. Can't deal with groups of people and tend to fixate on having one person meet their needs exclusively. No energy to hold up their side of a relationship, always dependent.

SPIRITUAL

Deficient. Can be very spiritual, but will turn over their soul to a guru or teacher in hopes of gaining salvation and oneness, especially any that speak about unconditional love. They may be very devout, wanting to go into the clergy or be a nun, but they don't follow through because they believe that God abandoned them in times of great need.

Getting Clear About Your Soul's Purpose for Success in Life

PHYSICAL APPEARANCE

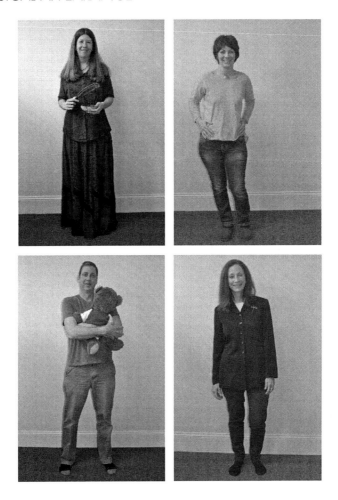

When you are visually assessing a person's Profile, notice that the Emotional Intelligence Specialist/ Poor Me appears gentle, often innocent. Their body tends to be soft and flexible, not defined or muscular, and their face is often childlike in its openness. Eyes are deep and compassionate and often watery, since Emotional Intelligence Specialists are never far from crying with either joy or pain in any moment. Their energy is pooled in the hips and heart area, both energetic centers of emotion. Their most salient traits are their sweetness and ability to love unconditionally. When you are around a person in this Profile, you feel the love.

CELEBRITY/MEDIA EXAMPLES

PRINCESS DIANA

POPE FRANCIS

TOM HANKS

HOW TO EMPOWER PEOPLE IN POOR ME DEFENSE

Being able to motivate someone who is stuck in self-sabotaging behaviors and attitudes is not easy, but it is so much easier when you know who you are dealing with and how they may sabotage themselves from being in defense. Emotional Intelligence Specialists in Poor Me Defense sabotage themselves by spending their energy trying to get others to fill their emotional needs, so they are overwhelmed, and exhausted, unable to deal with conflicts effectively.

Think of your clients, your family members, your friends and coworkers who might fit this Profile. You can help them to get out of defense and back to their balanced and resourceful state, their core soul self. Only when connected to their soul will they have what they want in life, not what their limited, defended self is providing.

Here are some ways to empower the Poor Mes in your life:
1. Never tell them to stop crying or suck it up.
2. Let them know you see their deep compassion and heart.
3. Remind them that their sensitivity is their greatest strength and makes them the most courageous people, not the weakest.
4. Sit quietly with them, but do not try to fix them.
5. Honor their overwhelm and hurt emotions but do not enable them by telling them they are justified in being hurt. Just hold space until they feel safe in having their feelings.

YOUR PERSONAL *Life Purpose Profile* WORKSHEET

Here is a chance for you to apply what you've learned. Answer the questions below to sharpen your vision of your own life's purpose and then be able to help others to do the same. Knowing your direction and mission is the key to having what you really want in life, today not tomorrow!

1. Do you see yourself in the description of this Profile, either in balance or in defense?

O YES!   O SOMEWHAT   O VERY LITTLE

> *(If you answered **Very Little**, then you want to read about the other four Profiles to find if another description fits better for you. Skip question #2 for now and answer question #4 on this worksheet about other people in your life.)*

2. If you answered *Yes* or *Somewhat* above, take a moment and write down how your Emotional Intelligence Specialist core quality supports you in your career, relationships and health. Then write how being in your Poor Me defense sabotages you in those same areas.

EMOTIONAL INTELLIGENCE SPECIALIST CORE SOUL QUALITY:

Career/Financial Freedom _____

Relationship Fulfillment _____

Vibrant Health and Well-being _____

POOR ME DEFENSE:

Career/Financial Freedom _____

Relationship Fulfillment _____

Vibrant Health and Well-being _____

Getting Clear About Your Soul's Purpose for Success in Life

3. Now write some steps you could take that would support you to live more in your core soul quality:

1 _____

2 _____

3 _____

4. Do you recognize people in your life that fit the qualities of this Profile, both balanced and in defense? If so, choose one specific person and write about **A)** the impact he or she has had on your life, and **B)** how you might best relate to that person to support them when they are in defense to be restored to balance.

A _____

B _____

MEET MY FRIEND EMILY...

I have another favorite person in my life, someone I think of as my most friendly friend—Emily.

Like my other friends, Emily may remind you of someone you know. She has a great smile and a warm heart, and is always there to lend a hand or give you a hug or high five when you've accomplished a goal and want some acknowledgment. She is also there with a shoulder to cry on when you've had a hard day or a sad loss.

Friendship is easy for Emily, as she loves people and people love her. She never forgets my birthday, always calls and has some kind of gift for me, even if I don't give her anything. Maybe you have a close friend who is like Emily, or maybe it's your mother, or your sister. It's that person in your life who never gives up on you.

Emily is a born mother and loves children. She may not be the most organized person, but she is the most caring and sacrificing for her family and those she takes care of—which is everyone! She is a top cook and baker, making treats that are always out of this world. Emily is the holiday cookie queen; she starts to bake two months before the big day and freezes everything wrapped and ready to go to ensure that everyone gets a gift of love from her.

Before you read on, ask yourself, do you know someone like my friend Emily Are you like her? Are you married to someone like Emily?

On her bad days, however, Emily feels unappreciated for all she does and thinks she should stop being such a sucker for a sad face. She hates the part of her that can't say no or says yes when she really doesn't have the time or energy to do what's being asked of her. Because Emily so often puts her own needs last, she attracts people who are "users" and take advantage of her good nature and support.

If you are like Emily, you never put your own life above your kids, spouse, or clients, or anyone who is having a problem. The way you give is so automatic and uncontrollable, you find yourself wanting to pull away from everyone and go live in a cave! But you never will because you love people, and you are miserable without them.

In her massage therapy business, my friend Emily has a hard time charging enough for her services. She knows she undercharges, leaving her clients happy but herself stressed and not having the life she deserves for all she does. She even gives discounts or freebies and then resents that she did later, when the favors are not returned.

You may know and love a person like Emily, and have them in your life already. Or deep inside, you may be very much like my friend yourself. Left over and unexpressed resentment would be a clue, as would sheer exhaustion for all the work you do selflessly for others.

In the *Rhys Method Life Purpose Profile System®*, we call a person like Emily a *Team Player*. When in the company of a Team Player, you feel seen and supported in whatever you are doing in your life. Even when you are dead wrong and won't admit it, Team Players stand by you, often with a smile and expressions of love. These are the people who do not ask to be in the spotlight but encourage others to go for it. On the Team Player's bad days, when they just can't say no to anyone and are drowning in feelings of abuse, we say that they are in *People Pleaser* defense.

Enjoy the Team Players who support you and whom you may be unknowingly taking for granted. Invite them out to dinner or remind them how much you appreciate having a friend like them. They do so much more for you and others than you can ever know. To learn more about them, and how you can support them, coach them, live with them and love them, read on for an in-depth description. You will also learn how to embrace these soul quality gifts within yourself and become aware of the devastating defensive behaviors that occur when we forget the truth of who we are.

THE TEAM PLAYER

with People Pleaser Defense

Getting Clear About Your Soul's Purpose for Success in Life

PROFILE DESCRIPTION

The Team Player Profile, in both light (balanced) and dark (defended) aspects is described below. You will see how the *core soul quality* of this Profile flows freely outward into the world or is distorted into a false self called the Profile's *defense.*

Your core soul quality is your individual essence, the eternal part of you that was there the day you were born and never changes. As your primary life energy, it radiates out from your center through six levels: feeling/sensation, emotional, action, mental, worldly, and spiritual.

But when that same energy of your core soul quality is diverted into your defense, you live life from a limited perspective and have no real power. Each of the five Life Purpose Profiles you will learn about reacts and goes into defense uniquely. Your defense is not who you are; rather it is the way you react when you have forgotten who you really are. Your path back to wholeness and balance, your natural state, is available through first identifying and then living in your own Life Purpose Profile.

TEAM PLAYERS YOU MAY KNOW *are the neighbor who knocks on the door with a pot of soup when you're dealing with a sick child but in defense won't ever let you reciprocate; the smiling clerk at the grocery store who always has something cheerful to say when you are checking out; or the co-worker who stays late at night getting the job done when all others have gone home and never makes a big deal about it.*

IN THEIR **CORE SOUL QUALITY**, the Team Player is always open, loving and supporting of others, knowing unequivocally that their soul's life purpose is to let other people experience being seen, heard, and loved. This is true in whatever job they take, whether as the person behind the cash register or giving massage, always taking care to make the other person feel great. They are usually smiling, and when they talk to you, it feels like a hug. The Team Player knows their deepest purpose through connecting to another's soul and finding how both can walk life's path together in any moment.

In defense, the *People Pleaser* doesn't know who they are as a soul or what their purpose is in life. This is because they are in resistance to people in their life and so can't get the soul message directly. They go into a relationship with the hope that another will tell them who they are. They often visit psychics to find out who they are and what they should do in life but never get what they are looking for, since the guidance they need is standing right in front of them.

AT THE FEELING LEVEL, Team Players are intuitive about other people's needs and will support them individually and emotionally. Rather than figuring out how to serve another, they recognize a person's needs intuitively and fill them. Every relationship they create in this way connects them to their warm and loving heart, creating the feelings that call them into the world and feed them.

In defense, *People Pleasers* block their own personal feelings and feel through others instead. They feel what the other is feeling, so they can know what to do in serving them, but not feel their own needs. You'll hear them say things like, *I see you need this...You're thirsty, can I get you a drink? How can I help you?*

AT THE EMOTIONAL LEVEL, Team Players are open-hearted, affectionate, happy, connected, fun and playful. They are steadfast and committed, very hard to fluster. As the Rock of Gibraltar, they are always reliable in their support, getting people elected to office, standing behind them 100%. They are believers, holding that space of faith and certainty for whomever they are serving. They are powerful, strong, willful space-holders in the world for everyone.

In defense, *People Pleasers* hold their emotions and self-expression tightly in, denying any personal needs. They follow this pattern sometimes for months before they get angry for not being appreciated and blow up at the people they want to serve. Then they feel another set of emotions: guilt and shame.

Emotionally, they will tend to have a narrow range of expression, limited to brooding anger (below the surface), resentment, guilt, shame and humiliation. They fear if they stand out as individuals, they'll get shot down and be humiliated, a situation they try to avoid at all cost.

People Pleasers will never confront another, but rather resort to passive resistance, meaning they say they'll do something and then not do it or not do it correctly. Their only sense of independence and power comes from *not doing* something they said they would do. When others get angry at them, People Pleasers assert their right to get angry in retaliation. *How dare you be angry at me now! I've sacrificed so much...* They don't feel they have the right to be angry on their own, only in response to another's anger.

AT THE ACTION LEVEL, Team Players can be depended upon and are extremely loyal. They are the people who know a job has to get done, and when all others leave, they stay and finish it. They have the stamina to do it and never blame others who leave for being wimpy or selfish. Knowing it's their purpose, they will never walk away from a commitment until it is completed. All of their actions are for people, not for the outcome, so they would never let another person down. They have clear boundaries and will not promise something they cannot and will not happily deliver.

In defense, *People Pleasers* provide service and spend their energy on others, leaving very little energy for themselves. They work all day then visit a neighbor in the evening and end up making dinner for the entire family because someone in that household is ill. It's a never-ending saga of service for the People Pleaser.

AT THE MENTAL LEVEL, Team Players are highly intelligent socially and have the ability to befriend almost anyone. At a party, they connect with everyone, and at the end of the evening everyone they have talked to feels seen, heard, understood and loved through their words. They have a great memory for names and details about people, and are able to remember someone's favorite food or hobby or their children's birthdays, even if they only see that person once a year. In service businesses, this is a million dollar skill, but unfortunately Team Players are not wired to care about the money.

In defense, the *People Pleasers'* creative vision of self is defined by others' beliefs and blocked with routine habits. They constantly look for someone else to tell them what to do because they think they are not very smart. They struggle with a society that says everyone should think for themselves, when in truth people often go along with what others think, which is mentally confusing for People Pleasers. They want others to tell them what to do, but when others do and their direction is self-serving, the People Pleaser gets resentful.

AT THE WORLDLY LEVEL, Team Players generally give themselves freely in support of others and the community. They are always part of a Food Bank or similar organization, doing anything they can to be a provider of service. They almost always have a service business, but even if they are in the corporate world, they give more than they take.

  In defense, *People Pleasers* are controlled and feel like they are slaves, over-burdened and not in partnership for service to the world. They seek to escape the world of people as a solution to their feelings of enslavement, sometimes choosing a spiritual path. But they find soon escaping doesn't work, because people are their life purpose, and they can't support people while meditating alone in a cave.

AT THE SPIRITUAL LEVEL, Team Players know God by being in relationship with each person, rather than through a connection "above." They are here to make the life for the rest of us survivable. They can handle a tough world, keep a smile on, and keep moving. When others are giving up, they encourage them to continue. They're strong enough to help others make this world a safe place to live in.

  In defense, for *People Pleasers*, serving God is the only option, being divine themselves is not. Religion is another service job. They have no time for spirituality because they are too busy relentlessly taking care of others. In church, they are the ones who are working, passing the plate around while others are praying. They never get to know God, only to do God's service.

THE TEAM PLAYER BALANCED SYSTEM
BULL'S EYE CHART

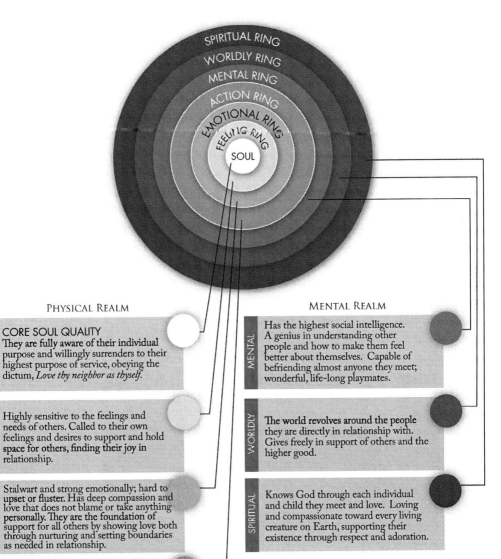

PHYSICAL REALM

SOUL

CORE SOUL QUALITY
They are fully aware of their individual purpose and willingly surrenders to their highest purpose of service, obeying the dictum, *Love thy neighbor as thyself.*

FEELING

Highly sensitive to the feelings and needs of others. Called to their own feelings and desires to support and hold space for others, finding their joy in relationship.

EMOTIONAL

Stalwart and strong emotionally; hard to upset or fluster. Has deep compassion and love that does not blame or take anything personally. They are the foundation of support for all others by showing love both through nurturing and setting boundaries as needed in relationship.

ACTION

Great stamina in actions and will persevere when others have lost all hope. They are the backbone of any family or business and will fully see all projects and missions through to completion. Becomes energized through the giving of services and taking care of those who need support, and so gives willingly through actions.

MENTAL REALM

MENTAL

Has the highest social intelligence. A genius in understanding other people and how to make them feel better about themselves. Capable of befriending almost anyone they meet; wonderful, life-long playmates.

WORLDLY

The world revolves around the people they are directly in relationship with. Gives freely in support of others and the higher good.

SPIRITUAL

Knows God through each individual and child they meet and love. Loving and compassionate toward every living creature on Earth, supporting their existence through respect and adoration.

THE PEOPLE PLEASER OUT OF BALANCE
BULL'S EYE CHART

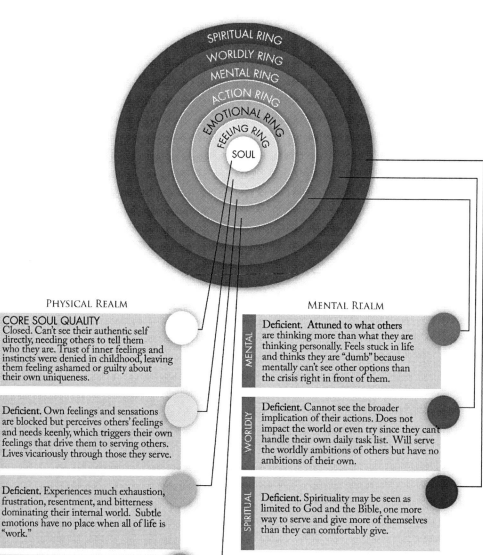

PHYSICAL REALM

SOUL
CORE SOUL QUALITY
Closed. Can't see their authentic self directly, needing others to tell them who they are. Trust of inner feelings and instincts were denied in childhood, leaving them feeling ashamed or guilty about their own uniqueness.

FEELING
Deficient. Own feelings and sensations are blocked but perceives others' feelings and needs keenly, which triggers their own feelings that drive them to serving others. Lives vicariously through those they serve.

EMOTIONAL
Deficient. Experiences much exhaustion, frustration, resentment, and bitterness dominating their internal world. Subtle emotions have no place when all of life is "work."

ACTION
Excessive. Always has one more job than can be handled gracefully while still maintaining a sense of self, staying in a constant state of exhaustion. Says things like, I have to do this, not I want to do this. Feels lost in the world without a service job that defines them. Uses passive resistance (like doing a job poorly), rather than disappointing others by saying no directly.

MENTAL REALM

MENTAL
Deficient. Attuned to what others are thinking more than what they are thinking personally. Feels stuck in life and thinks they are "dumb" because mentally can't see other options than the crisis right in front of them.

WORLDLY
Deficient. Cannot see the broader implication of their actions. Does not impact the world or even try since they can't handle their own daily task list. Will serve the worldly ambitions of others but have no ambitions of their own.

SPIRITUAL
Deficient. Spirituality may be seen as limited to God and the Bible, one more way to serve and give more of themselves than they can comfortably give.

Getting Clear About Your Soul's Purpose for Success in Life

PHYSICAL APPEARANCE

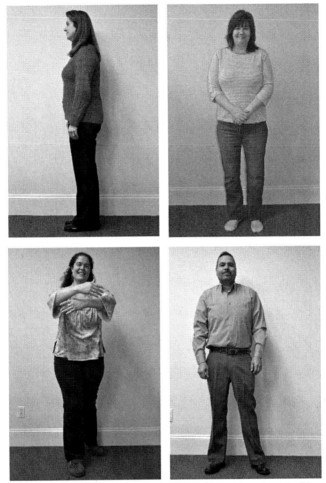

When you are visually assessing a person's Profile, notice that the Team Player/People Pleaser carries their energy in the belly and heart areas, making them seem warm and inviting. They may also be carrying extra weight in those areas of the body. Team Players give great hugs and have broad, open faces, smiling easily when they greet you. When you talk with them, their eyes rarely stray, showing how much they are connected and care about you. These people have huge hearts, giving you the feeling they are there for you, even more than they are for themselves. The Team Player's most salient traits are their solidly grounded compassion and attentiveness, making you feel deeply cared for by them as their very best friend.

MATA AMRITANANDAMAYI

ALAN HALE, JR. – "THE SKIPPER"

KEVIN JAMES

FLORENCE NIGHTINGALE

HOW TO EMPOWER PEOPLE IN PEOPLE PLEASER DEFENSE

Being able to motivate someone who is stuck in self-sabotaging behaviors and attitudes is not easy, but it is so much easier when you know who you are dealing with and how they may sabotage themselves from being in defense. Team Players in People Pleaser defense sabotage through never being able to saying no, being resentful, and being in abusive relationships where they are 80% responsible and their partner is 20%.

Think of your clients, your family members, your friends and coworkers who might fit this Profile. You can help them to get out of defense and back to their balanced and resourceful state, their core soul self. Only when connected to their soul will they have what they want in life, not what their limited, defended self is providing.

Here are some ways to empower the People Pleasers in your life:
1. Never tell them to just go it alone and start their own business. They must partner in the world to be successful.
2. Remind them how much they are appreciated.
3. Let them know that some people who take advantage of their good nature are not their friends, and it is okay to let them go.
4. Don't force them to tell you what they want to do, but instead give them options of things you can do together.

YOUR PERSONAL *Life Purpose Profile* WORKSHEET

Here is a chance for you to apply what you've learned. Answer the questions below to sharpen your vision of your own life's purpose and then be able to help others to do the same. Knowing your direction and mission is the key to having what you really want in life, today not tomorrow!

1. Do you see yourself in the description of this Profile, either in balance or in defense?

    ○ YES!   ○ SOMEWHAT   ○ VERY LITTLE

> *(If you answered **Very Little**, then you want to read about the other four Profiles to find if another description fits better for you. Skip question #2 for now and answer question #4 on this worksheet about other people in your life.)*

2. If you answered *Yes* or *Somewhat* above, take a moment and write down how your Team Player core quality supports you in your career, relationships and health. Then write how being in your People Pleaser defense sabotages you in those same areas.

TEAM PLAYER CORE SOUL QUALITY:

Career/Financial Freedom _____

Relationship Fulfillment _____

Vibrant Health and Well-being _____

PEOPLE PLEASER DEFENSE:

Career/Financial Freedom _____

Relationship Fulfillment _____

Vibrant Health and Well-being _____

Getting Clear About Your Soul's Purpose for Success in Life

3. Now write some steps you could take that would support you to live more in your core soul quality:

1 _____

2 _____

3 _____

4. Do you recognize people in your life that fit the qualities of this Profile, both balanced and in defense? If so, choose one specific person and write about **A)** the impact he or she has had on your life, and **B)** how you might best relate to that person to support them when they are in defense to be restored to balance.

A _____

B _____

MEET MY FRIEND ASHLEY...

Here is another one of my favorite people in life—her name is Ashley.

Ashley is a person that I have striven to be like my entire life, but I just don't have the kind of internal organization and self-discipline she so effortlessly demonstrates.

You may know someone like Ashley. She is graceful and fit, always appearing well-put together with not a hair out of place or wrinkle in her well-selected outfits (unless that is the look she is going for). In all areas of her life, there are systems and structures that hold everything neatly together.

Ashley has a soft heart for the down-trodden. She finds ways to help and support many people to get back on their feet and rise above their struggles to thrive in life. She sits on three boards of charitable organizations, and she's always the head of an organization's event or fundraising committee.

Ashley lives in a world where everything has a place and there is a place for everything. A recent advertisement from a big department stores appealed to the "Gift Giver" personality. Ashley is that person. She delivers her gifts wrapped perfectly, and they are always just what I need at the time I need it. Once she wrote out the instructions on how to use a new super-blender she gave me, so I wouldn't have to deal with the confusing directions on the box. Her attention to detail is, to me, stunning.

Ashley works hard and gets more done in one day than I could get done in a week, and still has time to take care of family, get her daily workouts in, throw great parties, and play with her cute doggie. Being around her is like being in a whirlwind of activity and accomplishment—she gets things done! If you know someone like her, you're probably envious, as am I, of their ability to accomplish so much.

Maybe you're starting to see your self in my friend Ashley. Whether she is managing a hundred people in a project or her own children getting homework done on time, she does it thoroughly and with integrity. Each

Getting Clear About Your Soul's Purpose for Success in Life

person she interacts with feels they are special and that she has tailored her help just for them.

Does this sound like you? Are you meticulous, never late, and always involved in making something happen? Do you take pride in finishing what you start and doing it in the best way you know possible, no matter what it is?

Maybe you know someone like Ashley. Does she remind you of your mother or father, or maybe your boss?

As capable as Ashley is, on her bad days she can be run by a ferocious slave driver, her inner critic that never acknowledging anything she does as good enough. She only accepts absolute perfection in whatever she does, says, and presents to the world.

Think of the people in your life who drive themselves beyond their limits day after day in an attempt to be perfect and achieve more than anyone else. At the same time, they expect those around them to have the same work ethic and discipline. If you've been around a person like Ashley, you might feel judged by them, while they think they are simply giving constructive criticism. Do you know any successful people like Ashley who seem to navigate through life gracefully and effortlessly, but at times are over-the-top demanding and often annoyingly nit-picky?

In the *Rhys Thomas Life Purpose Profile System®*, we call someone like Ashley the *Knowledgeable Achiever*. When you are in a relationship with a Knowledgeable Achiever, they see what you are capable of and they encourage you to reach for what you want in your life. They even give you tips on how to get there—ones you can use! They would never enable you in any way if they saw you sabotaging yourself, but their firmness and resolve can give you strength to challenge your own bad habits. On their bad days, when their inner critic gets the best of them and nothing they or anyone else does is good enough, we say that they are in *Rule Keeper* defense.

Enjoy the Knowledgeable Achievers in your life. Don't compete and strive to be like them, but rather let them support you in being even better than you are today. To learn more about them, and how you can support them, coach them, live with them and love them, read on for an in-depth description. You will also learn how to embrace these soul quality gifts within yourself and become aware of the devastating defensive behaviors that occur when we forget the truth of who we are.

PROFILE IV

THE KNOWLEDGEABLE ACHIEVER

with Rule Keeper Defense

www.RhysMethod.com | www.RhysThomasInstitute.com

PROFILE DESCRIPTION

The Knowledgeable Achiever Profile, in both light (balanced) and dark (defended) aspects is described below. You will see how the *core soul quality* of this Profile flows freely outward into the world or is distorted into a false self called the Profile's *defense*.

Your core soul quality is your individual essence, the eternal part of you that was there the day you were born and never changes. As your primary life energy, it radiates out from your center through six levels: feeling/sensation, emotional, action, mental, worldly, and spiritual.

But when that same energy of your core soul quality is diverted into your defense, you live life from a limited perspective and have no real power. Each of the five Life Purpose Profiles you will learn about reacts and goes into defense uniquely. Your defense is not who you are; rather it is the way you react when you have forgotten who you really are. Your path back to wholeness and balance, your natural state, is available through first identifying and then living in your own Life Purpose Profile.

KNOWLEDGEABLE ACHIEVERS YOU MAY KNOW *are the life coach who helps you stay on track and reach your goals, giving you exactly what you need to get the edge in your business, but sometimes gets bogged down in the details. The marathon runner friend who somehow finds time to train and compete in race after race while simultaneously driving a fundraising campaign for blind children but in defense is never satisfied that any of it is good enough. Or the husband or wife who manages the bills and other household business impeccably, freeing you to indulge your more creative pursuits, but is always hyper-critical of how you spend your time.*

IN THEIR **CORE SOUL QUALITY**, the Knowledgeable Achiever is the essence of genius and mastery. They are open to truth at every level and let themselves be guided by connecting to their inner light through their tender hearts and unified vision of the world, not just through logic. As a soul, they never effort to get somewhere; rather they simply live life, and every moment

Getting Clear About Your Soul's Purpose for Success in Life

in life is something that can be mastered. They know that true wisdom is not found in past knowledge but rather discovered in each moment, and they apply the lessons of the past to transform into new and more expanded awareness.

In defense, the *Rule Keeper* is deficient in awareness of their soul; they don't even acknowledge that they have one. The Rule Keeper already "knows" how things should go and so finds it inconvenient to have a soul guiding them or suggesting for example that their not-so-successful business may have fulfilled its spiritual purpose in their life, and it's now time to move on. Rule Keepers *are* what they *do*, needing no connection to an inner life or core essence.

AT THE FEELING LEVEL, Knowledgeable Achievers intuitively know the truth and accept the order, flow, and rhythm of life. They have a sense of what is right and trust how everything fits a plan they can see. They let people and events go through what is necessary to learn in the bigger picture, holding a perspective that includes it all. They don't get emotionally involved and stay back to let others find their path—a tough love approach they believe is the most loving thing anyone has ever done for the other person, helping that person stand on their own two feet. They are grounded in and can teach love, understanding the depth of non-judgmental justice.

In defense, *Rule Keepers* block their feelings in order to enhance their performance. Their constant mantra is, *I don't feel, I do.* They judge what is right and wrong, hardly tolerating any aberration, being rigid and not able to flow with life. They see someone making mistakes, struggling in life, and are quick to punish them if they go too far astray. They are only able to support that which fits the rules as "good;" otherwise it doesn't exist.

AT THE EMOTIONAL LEVEL, Knowledgeable Achievers feel broad emotions and struggles in all of humanity, knowing the world directly through primary states of being. They are strong, yet feel the vulnerability of their hearts, and through their hearts feel the struggles that others deal with in their complex emotions. Not gushers emotionally, they nevertheless have great enthusiasm for life, rising to challenges to celebrate their personal best at every opportunity, never fearing or doubting themselves in their endeavors.

In defense, *Rule Keepers* are limited to expressing appropriate emotions always staying on top of maintaining control. Emotions are only useful when they can be used to motivate them to achieve more. They must have some rational application in their lives if they are to be expressed at all.

Rule Keepers express basic emotions to fit all situations: contentment, sadness, frustration, detachment, focused, and interested. The emotional range is chosen to give the greatest opportunity for clarity in any situation. Overwhelming love and helpless depression don't enter the Rule Keepers more robotic existence. *Appropriate* is a word often used by the Rule Keeper; also, *I know.*

In matters of the heart, the Rule Keeper doesn't know how to let love in, so never truly knows love. Love for them is the amount of security they bring their family. It may be the gift of flowers they bring home on a holiday, the size of the diamond they buy for their spouse, or their efforts in driving the children to their sports and events. Without being able to love, they are never able to feel they are real and so must always prove they exist. They are driven to perform, building a bigger and better mask all day long, hoping to feel they are then real in some concrete way. But it isn't until their heart opens, until they let love in, that they actually do become real.

AT THE ACTION LEVEL, Knowledgeable Achievers excel, whether in sports or in any form of educational studies, seeing themselves as performance machines. They are strong and well-coordinated physically, with agile minds. Some may become great athletes in many arenas, while others acquire many degrees and letters behind their names. They love testing their skill against others, yet always keep a balance when in competition. They constantly push beyond their limits but know when to stop, rest, and recover.

Mastery-oriented, they want to be the best at whatever they do. They can take a business that is floundering and turn it around by putting people in the right positions after just meeting them for five minutes, seeing deeply into a person's core and how they fit in that company. They assess a person from the inside out, seeking to know what they are made of, how disciplined they are internally, and what's the truth about them. From there, they guide and teach anyone to attain their highest performance.

In defense, *Rule Keepers* are perfectionists who don't listen to their bodies in physical performance and will push themselves to the limit. Even so, they are never satisfied with any performance, always feeling they could do better. They can become champion athletes but take risks and undergo surgeries that land them in a wheel chair at age 40. They keep on going, just because they can, their motivation always being about their own personal aspirations and achievement.

In business, Rule Keepers will review a person's resume and assign any job as long as their background fits the job description. They strive to define that one unique quality of a person they can always count on, regardless of any sign that such a cookie cutter approach doesn't always work. They know exactly how things are going to go and judge others on external behavior, quick to label and then negate the person's deeper nature. For a Rule Keeper, life happens on the surface only in what can be seen and touched.

AT THE MENTAL LEVEL, Knowledgeable Achievers have sharp, intelligent minds, capable of grasping complex ideas, plans, schematics or other abstractions. They have the mental acuity and strength to see value in postponing emotional gratification for a much loftier goal that will lead to long term happiness. They are perpetual students, always accumulating more knowledge about the world and themselves. In the area of self-knowledge, they've often done therapy, and understand themselves psychologically and emotionally.

In defense, *Rule Keepers* are organized and pragmatic, giving them control over all that they do. Mentally, they are task-oriented, lacking a bigger context in their vision and tending to be super list-checkers. Their vast self-knowledge becomes one more thing to be right about, as they add it to their already carefully crafted and chiseled mask. No one can argue with them— they are just too good at perfecting their rigid forms, making themselves safe and acceptable.

Rule Keepers judge themselves and others on one scale: the success and failure scale. More success than failure, and the person or organization is seen as valuable. Less and the person is judged as less valuable. They live by society's standards and must be at the top of those standards. If not, they have a constant feeling of disappointment in themselves that drives them even harder to try once again to succeed.

AT THE WORLDLY LEVEL, Knowledgeable Achievers are high achievers in the world, competitive but always with an eye on what value they are here to share with the world. Achieving their personal best will always serve others by example. They strive to achieve at the highest level of success with balance of their spiritual, mental, and physical abilities and guide others to do the same. They are not seduced by striving for success or being right and use their mind and body to effortlessly reveal how to do things in the world that were previously thought to be impossible.

They are the true engineers (not the engin-NERDs) who are able to bring clarity to the most complex levels. They bring understanding into organizations, creating flowing, dynamic, and ever-changing structures to make them work. They easily manage large numbers of people, complex organizations and businesses, and they work exceptionally well in established arenas, such as corporations, governments, and financial institutions. They always know where the truth lies and can tell what's real, and what's fake. They are the great antique dealers who are able to tell the real McCoy from any imitation. They know how to find the light deep in the core of a person, and they are able to honor that core, the soul.

In defense, the *Rule Keeper* likes to be right, and would rather be right than happy. They are not "in the world," but rather in their own little world of striving which never lets up. Even when they are connecting with others, they are thinking about the jobs they should be doing in order to be successful. They constantly compete to measure who can achieve the highest in their area of expertise, preferring to stay aloof in personal relationships because their heart is off limits.

AT THE SPIRITUAL LEVEL, as the soul of the Knowledgeable Achiever matures, they become a sage (wise woman or wise man). This is not achieved through any accomplishment or expertise but through true mastery that is humble and flowing with wisdom, not facts. They live life fully and let each day unfold as their inspiration to create more, no longer investing energy into the iron-hard proofs of how life is. Instead, they surrender to universal truths to see the world as it really is, not as they would like it to be.

In defense, the *Rule Keeper* believes that spiritual expression is inconsequential and already knows God in a traditional, Biblical sense. They've taken five religious studies courses in college and have become an expert on God. But with denial of a soul self, they can never truly know God. They may also use the same strategy to dismiss spiritual reality altogether by becoming a scientist or doctor and seeing life as form rather than essence.

They may be very religious or a great spiritual achiever, owning yoga studios or writing great mystical books, but all their knowledge is based on written dogma, not on actual experience. They are highly opinionated and actually worship their own ideas as false gods. Whatever religion or spiritual practice they choose becomes the only true religion. They may be atheists or people who are rigidly attached to God as all mighty, all-seeing, and removed from daily affairs.

THE KNOWLEDGEABLE ACHIEVER BALANCED SYSTEM
BULL'S EYE CHART

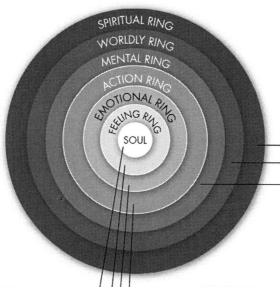

SPIRITUAL RING
WORLDLY RING
MENTAL RING
ACTION RING
EMOTIONAL RING
FEELING RING
SOUL

PHYSICAL REALM

SOUL
CORE SOUL QUALITY
Fully aware of being a soul first and a physical form second. Their soul becomes their primary guide in life, connecting them deeply to the Creator.

FEELING
Feels the flow, rhythm, and precision in all of life, even in what some may call failure. Has a very delicate heart that can be brought to tears by the subtlest sensation.

EMOTIONAL
Unconditionally open-hearted to let in people and the universe. Able to make the best of what they are given in any moment. Emotions drive their creative mind more than their mind drives emotions.

ACTION
Loves mastery in any form and is open to letting the universe move them with power and grace. Whether in business, athletics or relationships, what they do is an art that flows out of their actions and thoughts, as they effortlessly achieve their goal in all endeavors.

MENTAL REALM

MENTAL
Sees the big picture, not of structure and its weaknesses, but of the underlying spiritual purpose of any person or event. Uses their deep understanding of systems and patterns in math, science, literature, art, athletics as a base to allow the mind to be open to infinite possibility through intuitive channels.

WORLDLY
Achieves at the highest level of success in the world; balances spiritual, mental, and physical abilities and can guide others to do the same. Is not seduced by striving for success or being right. Uses mind and body to effortlessly reveal how to do things in the world that were thought to be impossible.

SPIRITUAL
Becomes a sage (wise woman or wise man) with maturity through the ripening of the soul, not through any accomplishment or expertise.

THE RULE KEEPER OUT OF BALANCE
BULL'S EYE CHART

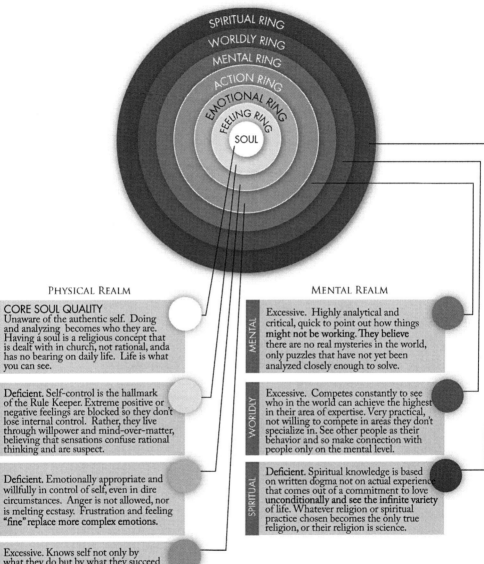

SPIRITUAL RING
WORLDLY RING
MENTAL RING
ACTION RING
EMOTIONAL RING
FEELING RING
SOUL

PHYSICAL REALM

SOUL

CORE SOUL QUALITY
Unaware of the authentic self. Doing and analyzing becomes who they are. Having a soul is a religious concept that is dealt with in church, not rational, and a has no bearing on daily life. Life is what you can see.

FEELING

Deficient. Self-control is the hallmark of the Rule Keeper. Extreme positive or negative feelings are blocked so they don't lose internal control. Rather, they live through willpower and mind-over-matter, believing that sensations confuse rational thinking and are suspect.

EMOTIONAL

Deficient. Emotionally appropriate and willfully in control of self, even in dire circumstances. Anger is not allowed, nor is melting ecstasy. Frustration and feeling "fine" replace more complex emotions.

ACTION

Excessive. Knows self not only by what they do but by what they succeed at. They are perfectionists and are rarely satisfied by any performance, always feeling they could do better and pushing themselves to limits that are inhuman.

MENTAL REALM

MENTAL

Excessive. Highly analytical and critical, quick to point out how things might not be working. They believe there are no real mysteries in the world, only puzzles that have not yet been analyzed closely enough to solve.

WORLDLY

Excessive. Competes constantly to see who in the world can achieve the highest in their area of expertise. Very practical, not willing to compete in areas they don't specialize in. See other people as their behavior and so make connection with people only on the mental level.

SPIRITUAL

Deficient. Spiritual knowledge is based on written dogma not on actual experience that comes out of a commitment to love unconditionally and see the infinite variety of life. Whatever religion or spiritual practice chosen becomes the only true religion, or their religion is science.

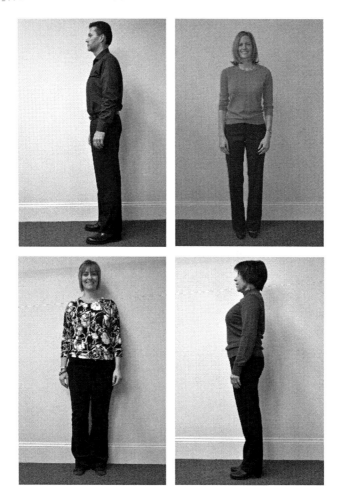

When you are visually assessing a person's Profile, notice that the Knowledgeable Achiever/Rule Keeper has perfect posture and an evenly balanced energy. They tend to be physically coordinated and rarely carry extra fat on their bodies. Knowledgeable Achievers look you straight in the eye and are not afraid of you looking as directly at them. They are proud of their bodies, displaying a self-confidence you can feel. These people are not huggers in general, but you sense they can meet you intellectually on almost any subject. Their most salient trait is their ability to manage their energy internally, making you feel safe in their presence.

CELEBRITY/MEDIA EXAMPLES

BILL GATES

HILLARY CLINTON

BARACK OBAMA

HOW TO EMPOWER PEOPLE IN RULE KEEPER DEFENSE

Being able to motivate someone who is stuck in self-sabotaging behaviors and attitudes is not easy, but it is so much easier when you know who you are dealing with and what to expect. Knowledgeable Achievers in Rule Keeper defense sabotage through their tough inner critic that is always disappointed in their own performance or success. They push themselves unmercifully.

Think of your clients, your family members, your friends and coworkers who might fit this Profile and its defense. You can help them get out of defense and back to their balanced and resourceful core soul state. Only then can they have what they really want in life, not what their limited, defended self is providing.

Here are some ways to empower the Rule Keepers in your life:
1. Remind them, when they are hyper-focused on the "one right and true way," that they can take a step back and see the bigger picture in any situation.
2. Let them decide if what they are doing now is going to lead to the happiness and success they truly want.
3. Have them take vacations and learn to enjoy non-productive time with family.
4. Challenge them to come up with a plan to balance both their personal needs and their goals and aspirations—they love the word "balance."

YOUR PERSONAL *Life Purpose Profile* WORKSHEET

Here is a chance for you to apply what you've learned. Answer the questions below to sharpen your vision of your own life's purpose and then be able to help others to do the same. Knowing your direction and mission is the key to having what you really want in life, today not tomorrow!

1. Do you see yourself in the description of this Profile, either in balance or in defense?

    O YES!   O SOMEWHAT   O VERY LITTLE

> *(If you answered **Very Little**, then you want to read about the other four Profiles to find if another description fits better for you. Skip question #2 for now and answer question #4 on this worksheet about other people in your life.)*

2. If you answered *Yes* or *Somewhat* above, take a moment and write down how your Knowledgeable Achiever core quality supports you in your career, relationships and health. Then write how being in your Rule Keeper defense sabotages you in those same areas.

KNOWLEDGEABLE ACHIEVER CORE SOUL QUALITY:

Career/Financial Freedom _____

Relationship Fulfillment _____

Vibrant Health and Well-being _____

RULE KEEPER DEFENSE:

Career/Financial Freedom _____

Relationship Fulfillment _____

Vibrant Health and Well-being _____

3. Now write some steps you could take that would support you to live
   more in your core soul quality:

1 _____

2 _____

3 _____

4. Do you recognize people in your life that fit the qualities of this Profile,
   both balanced and in defense? If so, choose one specific person
   and write about **A)** the impact he or she has had on your life, and
   B) how you might best relate to that person to support them when
   they are in defense to be restored to balance.

A _____

B _____

MEET MY FRIEND ANTHONY...

And finally, I want to introduce you to Anthony, my friend who demonstrates a particular quality that he shares with many others like him.

As with my soft and gentle friend Lynda, whom I introduced to you earlier, I have stood in harsh judgment of people like Anthony. In sports, I'd often be pitted against someone like him in verbal and even physical battles and could never win. At the same time, I wanted to be more like him—which I would never admit!

You may know someone like Anthony. He is strikingly handsome, strong, and outgoing, exuding a kind of charisma that makes him attractive regardless of his appearance. He tends to be good at whatever he sets his mind to do, always achieving his goal in half the time I take to do the same thing. Do you know a winner like Anthony, someone who seems like a natural at whatever he or she does?

He has a tough, impenetrable exterior, but those select people he admits into his inner sanctum know he has a soft side. He is very emotional but hides this vulnerability from people until he knows them well enough to trust them with his more tender emotions. He's the kind of guy who would always have your back if he thinks you might be in trouble.

Maybe you're seeing yourself in Anthony. Are you tough on the outside but a secret softy when you find someone you can trust as a lover or friend?

Anthony fights injustice and is fearless when it comes to staring down, dressing down, or even beating down a person who he believes is untrustworthy. He is not afraid of aggression and coercion, and will get into physical fights if necessary, although he much prefers diplomacy. He's a born leader and gets others to make the right choices without using force but rather by inspiring them to act.

Anthony's charm is contagious. He loves people and they love him. As good-looking as he is, it is his magnetic ability to look deep into you when he talks to you that makes him so appealing. You might have a tiny inkling of a thought that Anthony is like you. If so, you might be quick to deny it, because being someone like Anthony isn't easy. Of all my favorite people, Anthony's particular qualities are the hardest to own and live up to. Stepping into Anthony's shoes can be risky and dangerous, but the kind of leadership he provides is so very needed in the world today. Are you like him but cautious to admit it?

Whatever line of work he is in, Anthony is always being the quintessential salesman. He's so good, he could sell ice to Eskimos! But he wouldn't unless it was what they truly wanted. Rather, he sells with a deeper commitment of helping the customer truly get what they want. Anthony will walk away empty-handed if he deems that someone doesn't need what he's selling.

On his bad days, Anthony can be your worst nightmare, especially when he loses his temper. Or worse, he can be his own worst enemy and self-saboteur. He's good at making money and having relationships that support him, but he can also destroy whatever he creates in the blink of an eye by going into battle with co-workers, staff, and family, or by just being too impulsive and reckless in his personal affairs.

Does my description remind you of a child, a parent or a spouse who is like Anthony? Think of the drama kings and queens in your life, the ones who don't hesitate to unleash their emotions in full Technicolor, often for effect in getting what they want, although they'd never admit it. When was the last time someone you know "flipped out" when they were cornered or forcibly asked to do something they didn't want to do?

You may be attracted to a person like Anthony but afraid to get too close. People like Anthony can be seductive as romantic partners but highly demanding of your energy and devotion. It's an all or nothing affair—there's no standing on the sidelines when you are involved in the life of someone like Anthony.

In the *Rhys Method Life Purpose Profile System®*, we honor the qualities of my friend Anthony by calling those who are like him the *Charismatic Leader-Charmer*. When you are around people like Anthony, their energy and strength seems to rub off on you, and you want to be like them. All great leaders and actors have the qualities of the Charismatic Leader-Charmer. Wherever they go, they tend to be catalysts for change, inspiring and motivating others to also become "change agents" in the world. On their bad days, Charismatic Leader-

Charmers can be highly controlling and manipulative, not hesitating to use force against those they decide are their enemies, making them dangerous to be around. When in that mode, we say that they are in *Enforcer-Seducer* defense.

Think about the people in your life who have inspired you to reach further and find the energy to make a difference in the world. Think also about the people who have pushed you or hurt you through their aggression or belligerence in such a way that you had to stand up for yourself and set clear boundaries. Either way, a Charismatic Leader-Charmer got you out of your comfort zone and caused you to become a better person than you were before.

Enjoy the charismatic and charming people in your life. Worship them and let them inspire you to be even greater than you thought you ever could be. To learn more about them, and how you can support them, coach them, live with them and love them, read on for a more in-depth description. You will also learn how to embrace these soul quality gifts within yourself and become aware of the devastating defensive behaviors that occur when we forget the truth of who we are.

THE CHARISMATIC LEADER-CHARMER

with Enforcer–Seducer Defense

Getting Clear About Your Soul's Purpose for Success in Life

PROFILE DESCRIPTION

The Charismatic Leader-Charmer Profile, in both light (balanced) and dark (defended) aspects is described below. You will see how the *core soul quality* of this Profile flows freely outward into the world or is distorted into a false self called the Profile's *defense*.

Your core soul quality is your individual essence, the eternal part of you that was there the day you were born and never changes. As your primary life energy, it radiates out from your center through six levels: feeling/sensation, emotional, action, mental, worldly, and spiritual.

But when that same energy of your core soul quality is diverted into your defense, you live life from a limited perspective and have no real power. Each of the five Life Purpose Profiles you will learn about reacts and goes into defense uniquely. Your defense is not who you are; rather it is the way you react when you have forgotten who you really are. Your path back to wholeness and balance, your natural state, is available through first identifying and then living in your own Life Purpose Profile.

> CHARISMATIC LEADERS YOU MAY KNOW *include those larger-than-life people who always seem to be the center of attention because of their heroic deeds; a spouse who demands your utmost loyalty yet in defense takes advantage of your generosity; the man (or woman) in a Hollywood movie who emerges from being the underdog and courageously saves the day against all odds; the sometimes charming or seductive person you admire from afar but are careful not to spend too much time around.*

IN THEIR **CORE SOUL QUALITY**, Charismatic Leader-Charmers are heroes. They are the powerful leaders, warriors, protectors, and actors born into a world that supports and serves them in their mission. They are not afraid to stand up for who they are and what they stand for, and never play down or pretend to be smaller than they are. They inspire others to do the same.

In defense, the *Enforcer-Seducer* is vulnerable in relationship to their soul and holds back from expressing their authentic self. They may disown their entitlement when seen by others as a "spoiled brat," and never fully acknowledge how they are supported in their core self, thus hiding their truth. This results in the Enforcer becoming a behind-the-scenes manipulator, unable to show their true leader quality. Such hiding also allows them to act without conscience and have no true remorse for harmful deeds to others.

AT THE FEELING LEVEL, Charismatic Leader-Charmers are intuitively sensitive to others' intentions and impending actions, and act instantly from their gut. In martial arts, they may move their hand in one direction not knowing why, and suddenly it meets a kick and stops it. They are so in tune with the energy field around them that they become one with it. In a verbal debate or argument, the Charismatic Leader is always one step ahead of their opponent, feeling the other's energy and becoming one with it. In a board room, they can deal with any situation and never get flustered; they are solid and present.

In defense, *Enforcer-Seducers* are hyper-vigilant to subtle changes in their environment or other people, constantly assessing the possibility of a threat to what they consider "theirs." They trust no one and feel that others are victimizers, justifying an emotional first-strike option. They are sensitive, but their sensitivity is excessive and fear-based, keeping them in a fortress of their own defense, always on guard.

Enforcer-Seducers often use the Poor Me defense, truly feeling they are broken and a victim which then justifies severe self-sabotage, addictions, and other life dramas. They have no remorse for their emotional outbursts or over-reactions, since it is always in response to what is someone else's fault. Their super sensitivity causes them to take everything personally so they will hang on to grudges and seek revenge. A typical Enforcer attitude is, *You betrayed me, so I will never trust you again. I am going to get even, one way or the other.*

AT THE EMOTIONAL LEVEL, Charismatic Leader-Charmers feel a full range of emotion and have no problem expressing a passion for freedom, power, and action. They trust what they are feeling and let their emotions guide them to act. There is never anything fake or weak about their emotional expression, which, when coming from a place of leadership to large groups has the authenticity that moves people to rise up and make lasting change in a society or nation. Passions flow freely as do all the emotions but always in balance and clean.

In defense, the *Enforcer-Seducer* is emotionally excessive, using emotions as tools to get compliance from others, not for expressing truth. The main three emotions Enforcers express on regular basis are anger, rage, and seduction. Enforcers are the drama kings and queens who will stop at nothing to manipulate a situation to their advantage with their excessive emotional expression. Or they use emotions to challenge and escape authority. You may have tried to get your school-age child to sit down and do their homework, and had them flip out, screaming and crying for an hour to avoid ever opening a book—sure signs of the Enforcer Profile. For them, emotions are functional, designed to indirectly achieve an end.

AT THE ACTION LEVEL, Charismatic Leader-Charmers' actions are powerful and graceful in every area of life. A fireman runs into a burning building without ever thinking about it; a soldier jumps on a live grenade because that's what needed to be done—these are the Charismatic Leaders in action, often exhibiting a fearlessness that signals they will die for their cause. Their reactions are visceral, carried out without need for a reason or rationale.

In defense, *Enforcer-Seducers* go through cycles of intense activity and then collapse or quit, often destructively. They become easily bored if not being entertained or focused on enough by those around them and then move on abruptly, sometimes vindictively, after having sabotaged themselves and burned too many bridges to ever return.

AT THE MENTAL LEVEL, thinking and acting are done instantaneously by Charismatic Leader-Charmers. They have a broad awareness, and are present-minded and intuitive. They are good at assessing opportunities for themselves and others, and don't hesitate to make a move if changing jobs or partners are seen to be of benefit. There is no love lost, no regret, as they go smoothly and effortlessly from one situation to the next, never accumulating baggage or leaving negativity in their wake. Their thinking is very efficient; once a plan is realized, they act on it fearlessly.

In defense, *Enforcer-Seducers* are constantly in a mental battle for control with the world and with people in their lives, always a few steps ahead of their opponent. They know how things are going to go, for better or worse, even before anything begins. In verbal, physical, and emotional battles, the Enforcer is ruthless, always getting the final word in or delivering a final blow that no one sees coming.

Enforcers trust no one, so it is only a matter of time until they see everyone as the enemy and enter into battle with them. Often, they are managing battles in multiple areas of their lives: at the office, in the bedroom, anywhere they can put up a fight in order to assert dominance or control. Beating others down mentally is how the Enforcer gets compliance and control.

AT THE WORLDLY LEVEL, Charismatic Leader-Charmers are leaders of people, fighting for justice, championing causes, and taking risks when needed. They surrender to their humanity and become public servants who stimulate true change for the better. They inspire and motivate others to act and are willing to die for their cause if it will create a powerful change in the world, as did Martin Luther King, Jr. They are the change agents in the world. Surprisingly, these Charismatic Leaders make up about one-third of the total population of our planet but are often invisible as they suppress their highest purpose for personal gain. In their hearts, however, they are here to fearlessly commit to fighting the good fight and inspire others.

In defense, the *Enforcer-Seducers* are excessive, challenging the world and those in it for who can gain the most control. It doesn't matter if it's getting a good parking place or creating a trumped up war that disguises a plan to gain the oil rights to an entire country's resources, Enforcers can be ruthless in their pursuits.

The Enforcer quality is more common than the core quality expression of Charismatic Leader, often being found in law, politics, and mindless corporations where they are attracted because those occupations offer opportunities for the most power and control. For example, an Enforcer will take a job and attempt to manipulate the boss, or use charm to rally the workers against the boss. They either win and quit, leaving devastation in their wake, or they get fired and then sue for unjust dismissal.

Enforcers can't trust others to lead them, so following others' directives is a real problem for them. Whether at work or in relationships, they tend to have about a four year period before they destroy everything they've built.

AT THE SPIRITUAL LEVEL, Charismatic Leader-Charmers embody the warrior hero, harnessing the creative force of the universe to lead others. They are surrendered to God, fully embodying universal forces of destruction and creation within themselves. They are free of attachments and willing to create newness in every moment, guided by their soul.

In defense, God is something *Enforcer-Seducers* use as a tool for controlling others, never surrendering because that would only mean defeat. They have strong spiritual egos and do battle to claim superiority as channels, gurus, or spiritual guides. Examples are TV evangelist Jimmy Swaggart and radio psychics who use spirituality as a ticket to accumulate personal riches. For the Enforcer, spirituality and religion are all about power and manipulation, only useful in making him or her "the chosen one" and therefore above all others and beyond reproach.

THE CHARISMATIC LEADER-CHARMER BALANCED SYSTEM
BULL'S EYE CHART

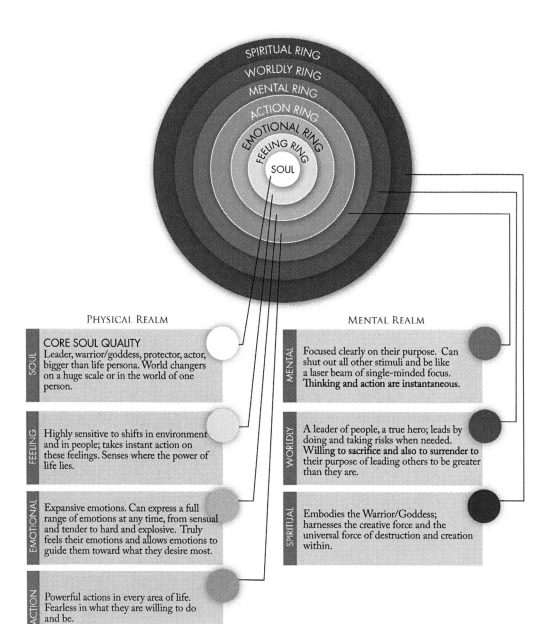

PHYSICAL REALM

CORE SOUL QUALITY
SOUL — Leader, warrior/goddess, protector, actor, bigger than life persona. World changers on a huge scale or in the world of one person.

FEELING — Highly sensitive to shifts in environment and in people; takes instant action on these feelings. Senses where the power of life lies.

EMOTIONAL — Expansive emotions. Can express a full range of emotions at any time, from sensual and tender to hard and explosive. Truly feels their emotions and allows emotions to guide them toward what they desire most.

ACTION — Powerful actions in every area of life. Fearless in what they are willing to do and be.

MENTAL REALM

MENTAL — Focused clearly on their purpose. Can shut out all other stimuli and be like a laser beam of single-minded focus. Thinking and action are instantaneous.

WORLDLY — A leader of people, a true hero; leads by doing and taking risks when needed. Willing to sacrifice and also to surrender to their purpose of leading others to be greater than they are.

SPIRITUAL — Embodies the Warrior/Goddess; harnesses the creative force and the universal force of destruction and creation within.

THE ENFORCER-SEDUCER OF BALANCE
BULL'S EYE CHART

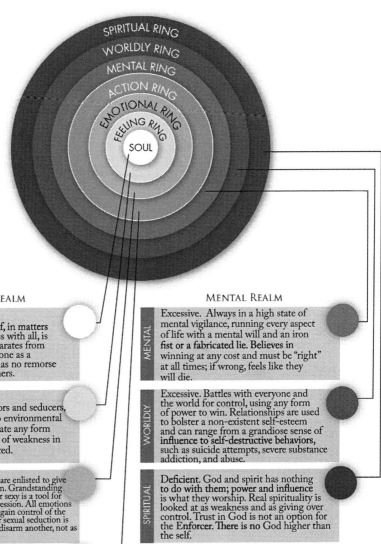

PHYSICAL REALM

SOUL

CORE SOUL QUALITY
Closed. The authentic self, in matters of conscience and oneness with all, is denied. The Enforcer separates from their soul in seeing everyone as a potential enemy and so has no remorse in their dealings with others.

FEELING

Excessive. As born warriors and seducers, they are hyper-vigilant to environmental changes that might indicate any form of danger or to any sense of weakness in others that can be exploited.

EMOTIONAL

Excessive. Emotional states are enlisted to give power to acts of manipulation. Grandstanding and acting hurt or enraged or sexy is a tool for manipulation, not a real expression. All emotions are aggressively expressed to gain control of the environment; even sensual or sexual seduction is used to elicit an outcome or disarm another, not as a spontaneous gesture.

ACTION

Excessive. Constantly in a state of survival-of-the-fittest, with no connection to the well-being of others. Challenges and battles the world for superiority and control, or vehemently rejects any participation in life, going on permanent disability and in and out of rehab. Can become useless and needy, or against everything as a way to control family and friends who see their potential. All their actions and non-actions are directed towards controlling others.

MENTAL REALM

MENTAL

Excessive. Always in a high state of mental vigilance, running every aspect of life with a mental will and an iron fist or a fabricated lie. Believes in winning at any cost and must be "right" at all times; if wrong, feels like they will die.

WORLDLY

Excessive. Battles with everyone and the world for control, using any form of power to win. Relationships are used to bolster a non-existent self-esteem and can range from a grandiose sense of influence to self-destructive behaviors, such as suicide attempts, severe substance addiction, and abuse.

SPIRITUAL

Deficient. God and spirit has nothing to do with them; power and influence is what they worship. Real spirituality is looked at as weakness and as giving over control. Trust in God is not an option for the Enforcer. There is no God higher than the self.

When you are visually assessing a person's **Profile**, notice that the Charismatic Leader-Charmer/Enforcer-Seducer has a dynamic energy that is magnetic. They can be sensually seductive and alluring, and often love to be in front of a camera or on stage. Their body shape will often take the form of their secondary Profile, so they can be overweight or underweight depending on what that Profile is. Their skin and musculature often has an elastic quality, allowing them to go from being out-of-shape to in-shape in a matter of weeks. Charismatic Leader-Charmers often have hourglass bodies with wide shoulders and a thin waist. They are eye-catching in appearance, even if not classically beautiful (which they often are) and have a charisma that captivates your attention. Their most salient traits are their fearlessness and sensuality, and their ability to inspire you just by being around them.

Getting Clear About Your Soul's Purpose for Success in Life

CELEBRITY/MEDIA EXAMPLES

OPRAH WINFREY

ANGELINA JOLIE

MARTIN LUTHER KING, JR.

HOW TO EMPOWER PEOPLE IN ENFORCER-SEDUCER DEFENSE

Being able to motivate someone who is stuck in self-sabotaging behaviors and attitudes is not easy, but it is so much easier when you know who you are dealing with and what to expect. Charismatic Leaders-Charmers in Enforcer-Seducer defense sabotage through not trusting anyone out of fear of betrayal, or through their own aggression or battling for control, or through hiding behind of any of the other Profile defenses, especially the Poor Me.

Think of your clients, your family members, your friends and co-workers who might fit this Profile and its defense. You can help them to get out of defense and back to their balanced and resourceful core soul state. Only then can they have what they really want in life, rather than what their limited self is providing.

Here are some ways to empower the Enforcer-Seducers in your life:
1. Remind them that they are truly a leader and have to decide what they are for not against.
2. Remind them that they are great fighters against injustice, but help them see that if they fight for what they don't want, they will get what they don't want.
3. Tell them when they are depressed or angry to go out and be social by talking to anyone, such as store clerks, people at a bus stop, etc.
4. Make it okay for them to live in four-year cycles of change. They are the change agents in the community and world, and like to shake things up every four years.

YOUR PERSONAL *Life Purpose Profile* WORKSHEET

Here is a chance for you to apply what you've learned. Answer the questions below to sharpen your vision of your own life's purpose and then be able to help others to do the same. Knowing your direction and mission is the key to having what you really want in life, today not tomorrow!

1. Do you see yourself in the description of this Profile, either in balance or in defense?

   O YES!   O SOMEWHAT   O VERY LITTLE

   *(If you answered **Very Little**, then you want to read about the other four Profiles to find if another description fits better for you. Skip question #2 for now and answer question #4 on this worksheet about other people in your life.)*

2. If you answered Yes or Somewhat above, take a moment and write down how your Charismatic Leader-Charmer core quality supports you in your career, relationships and health. Then write how being in your Enforcer-Seducer defense sabotages you in those same areas.

CHARISMATIC LEADER-CHARMER CORE SOUL QUALITY:

Career/Financial Freedom _____

Relationship Fulfillment _____

Vibrant Health and Well-being _____

ENFORCER-SEDUCER DEFENSE:

Career/Financial Freedom _____

Relationship Fulfillment _____

Vibrant Health and Well-being _____

3. Now write some steps you could take that would support you to live more in your core soul quality:

1 _____

2 _____

3 _____

4. Do you recognize people in your life that fit the qualities of this Profile, both balanced and in defense? If so, choose one specific person and write about **A)** the impact he or she has had on your life, and **B)** how you might best relate to that person to support them when they are in defense to be restored to balance.

A _____

B _____

CREATING PROFILE BALANCE

We all have one primary Life Purpose Profile. You may need to take some time to clearly see the one you have and fully embrace it. The key to knowing your Profile is that the core soul quality of that Profile has been with you since you were born; it is not some behavior you picked up in order to better deal with life. Also, it isn't your actions alone, either. Rather your primary Profile is something you must feel and be able to identify in both defense and in your core throughout your life.

Keep in mind that to be balanced and authentic, you must also embrace the other four Profiles and their core soul qualities within you, even if those others are only bit players in the choices you make. The blend of all five is what gives your highest quality its unique flavor and expression.

A word of caution: Your primary Profile never serves the other four, but rather the other four serve your primary Profile. You may have lived much of your life (as I did) in your secondary Profile, but no matter how good you get at living from that place, it will never fully feed you in your true life purpose. The more integrated you are internally, the more restored you are to your natural essence and power in life, and the less your defensive mode is needed. When you embrace the qualities within you that you may have rejected or did not see as good, you see that you have also rejected all the people in the world with that same trait. When you open to all of your traits and let them support you personally, all those relationships you struggled with transform to support your life and business, rather than appear to conflict with it, as well.

Read below about how each of the five Life Purpose Profiles brings balance through their core soul qualities to the others. Find the Profile you have identified as your own—or as someone else in your life—and begin to see how the awakening of that Profile's soul qualities can restore balance and take you and others out of a defensive mode.

I. CREATIVE IDEALISTS inspire balance in the other four Profiles in the following ways:

Knowledgeable Achievers stop being so nitpicky and begin to see not only the big picture of how things work in their immediate surroundings, but how things works more universally for everyone.

Emotional Intelligence Specialists realize that their feelings are infinite and that is their greatest gift.

Team Players see an infinite number of ways to serve others and come to love them all.

Charismatic Leader-Charmers become aware of the fears people have and how their job is to protect people and make them feel safe. They bring infinite wisdom, creativity, and opportunity to every one of the other Profiles.

II. EMOTIONAL INTELLIGENCE SPECIALISTS inspire balance in the other four Profiles in the following ways:

Creative Idealists are able to feel their thoughts, not just think them. They expand out from their world of megabytes and data to become more solid in the world. Einstein could think mathematically about light, but he could also feel himself riding on a beam of light, leading to his greatest discoveries.

Knowledgeable Achievers feel their hearts and realize how important people are; people aren't simply objects and doers, but real human beings.

Team Players learn to love themselves at a deep level. They don't need relationship, but may desire relationship, because they recognize that love is already who they are.

Charismatic Leader-Charmers gain a beautifully seductive quality, the ability to merge with another without invading. They can experience their soft emotional nature to support and empower others through connecting with them more deeply.

III. TEAM PLAYERS inspire balance in the other four Profiles in the following ways:

Creative Idealists are reminded that their crazy ideas can actually help people. They realize their ideas are not abstractions but channeled through from higher realms to better people's lives.

Knowledgeable Achievers see how important it is for them to help people find their way in a large organization. They see the importance of people getting along for ultimate success.

Emotional Intelligence Specialists can give their love without expecting to have it returned. They waken to the reality that giving alone is wonderful and realize they've been giving themselves the love they want from others the whole time.

Charismatic Leader-Charmers see the true value of people and become true leaders. They become people that others want to follow because people know they will die for them.

Until the Team Player awakes in Charismatic Leader-Charmers, no one will follow them. They are still leaders in their quality but are totally alone, an isolated person walking around telling others what to do, getting frustrated, and finally quitting.

IV. KNOWLEDGEABLE ACHIEVERS inspire balance in the other four Profiles in the following ways:

Creative Idealists get more grounded, having their thoughts and ideas come into the world in a solid way. Products get created, not just ideas.

Emotional Intelligence Specialists learn to have boundaries. They are able to distinguish between their own emotions and those of others, permitting them to act more reliably on their inner guidance.

Team Players learn discipline in choosing whom to serve and whom to quit serving. They are better able to set boundaries and so become less vulnerable to resentment.

Charismatic Leader-Charmers learn discipline to go along with their charisma and become impossible to stop. This combination of Knowledgeable Achiever and Charismatic Leader-Charmer is the dynamic duo, a powerful force capable of changing the world.

V. CHARISMATIC LEADER-CHARMERS inspire balance in the other four Profiles in the following ways:

When the Charismatic Leader-Charmer awakens in any of the Profiles, a person is empowered to be who they truly are. They are then willing to stand up and fully express who they are, unleashing their deepest soul quality into the world. The unbending and non-negotiable quality of the Charismatic Leader-Charmer supports people in all Profiles to stand firmly and securely, knowing they are living their truth and that their truth is worth fighting for.

Charismatic Leader-Charmers are the people who teach you how to be who you are as expressed by your unique Profile qualities. Hang out with them! They will show you what you need to embrace in order to become your own courageous hero.

WHAT THIS WORK MEANS FOR YOUR LIFE

Becoming a master of the Life Purpose Profiles is easy. Just practice talking to the core soul quality in everyone you meet. Practice seeing beyond their defense to the greatness within them. People are your mirror. When you can do this for 50 to 100 people you will also be able to see those incredible traits within yourself. You will begin to love and connect with people in the world in a way that only the most successful and happy people in the world do—openly, intelligently and compassionately. When you have done this for a 1000 to 10,000 people in your business, you will find that you will own your market and be the #1 resource in any industry or business you are in.

Why? Because, people don't really want you to sell them anything, or just be nice and give them something; they want you to see who they really are, what they are really capable of, and what they really need and want. When you can do that you don't need to tell them what their Profile is or even how you so brilliantly got to the bottom of their problem. You just inspire them to see more of themselves. When you help others to see their greatness in your own unique way, you are living your life purpose directly. You will have financial freedom from a career that embodies your gifts, you will have wonderful friends and loyal customers, and you will have the energy and health to enjoy your life for a long time to come.

Here is a powerful testimonial from one of my students that speaks to this:

"When I entered the Rhys Thomas Institute, I wanted to work on me as a person. I was tired of not being happy and at peace, totally isolated and working all the time. I was always trying to make everyone happy and getting angry in the process. As a holistic practitioner, I was taught that the more I worked on my own issues the better I would be able to do my work.

I had been working on myself for over 10 years and had gone through a second divorce when I entered the school. Through the school, I learned how I sabotaged myself by playing a People Pleaser most of my life instead of the Charismatic Leader that Rhys pointed out I am the first weekend in class. In learning the Life Purpose Profiles, I began to understand why I was behaving the way I was, and how to truly step into my power. I did the work to change old patterns and met the love of my life that I could never have even seen before I knew the Profiles.

My friends have noticed how much I have changed and like the new me way better than the old! My bodywork business now is not 'work,' but instead is fun and feeds both me and my clients. When they walk in to my office, I already know so much about how to help them even beyond the pain in their body. I now know that the pain in their body comes from forgetting who they really are at a very deep level. Because of the Profiles, I now can support them in not only relieving chronic pain but in making life choices that keep them healthier and happier. Clients will say to me, How do you know so much about me, and that I needed just that push in my life? They think I'm psychic, but I have just mastered the Profiles and can see the best in them at any moment—it's an incredible gift to me and to them."

MADDY ELIA, Owner of Integrated Body Health

HOW YOU CAN GO DEEPER IN THIS WORK

You've just gotten an amazing window on how we teach the Life Purpose Profiles at the Rhys Thomas Institute of Energy Medicine in the first year of the school's three-year program. I want to encourage you to take what you've learned and go as deep as you can with it, and I'm going to tell you how you can do that.

If you're a business person, a teacher, a coach, healer or doctor—whatever you do with people already—then you can add to your system a new dimension of understanding the life purpose of the people who come to you. You can remind them of their highest calling, their core soul quality that is naturally theirs since the day they were born. You can work with them to free up their defenses, opening the channels for their soul's primary life energy to radiate out through all levels of their lives. Working this way one-on-one with people enables them to understand the qualities they contribute to the world that are so desperately needed, and thus helps everyone.

What a gift to have such rapport with people, and then also be able to give them this gift! And the bonus is that for every person you interact with and understand through their Life Purpose Profile, you simultaneously understand those qualities deeper in yourself. You start loving people more, judging them less.

NEXT STEPS

Now that you've had a taste of what we do at our school, I encourage you to visit our website and take the free online Profile Assessment. In it, you respond to statements that bring you into clarity about who you are and what your life purpose is. If you recognized yourself in the Profiles I've described in this book, you'll get a deeper understanding of how your primary, secondary and other soul qualities combine to give you a fuller picture of who you are.

Other products available on my RhysMethod.com website include a DVD product entitled *The Rhys Method Life Purpose Profile System*® that shows you how I teach the Profile System® at the school in the first year. Also available is the DVD product, *The 12 Gateways to Your Life Purpose*, which introduces the 12 energy centers (7 chakras and 5 spiritual centers) we teach at the same time as we teach the Profile System®. Awareness of the 12 energy centers enables you to use the Law of Attraction for your unique life purpose, enhancing and expanding your ability to create what you desire in your life. Everything in life starts making sense when you combine these two elements, and both are available on my website.

A next step is to enroll in the Rhys Thomas Institute for Energy Medicine. At the school, we offer year round online training and five retreat weekends in which you work with groups of people to totally own your power and courage, and develop your ability to see and work with Profiles in a transformational way. You learn to see people's greatness, their highest qualities. If you want to go to next level, you can also get involved in our high-end coaching programs which support you in the daily application of these powerful systems.

This book is an introduction, a taste of a system that can make you the master of your life. How would you like to live your life with no excuses, full of love and really making a difference in the world? I will bet that when you get out of your defense that has kept you stuck and blocked from feeling your true calling, that you might just be pulled to join us for the journey of your life.

What would it be like if you were called to your life from an undeniable inner source, living your passion to the fullest every day of your life? Find out by enrolling in the Rhys Thomas Institute of Energy Medicine and begin to develop a deep self-awareness, compassion for others, and reverence for your life and your purpose. Everyone who does this becomes a transformative element, inspiring everyone else to step in and do the same. This is how we transform the world. This is what true energy medicine is all about. Awaken first from within you the pure energy of the soul, then share your brilliance with others, so they can do the same. The greatest leaders in the world like Martin Luther King did exactly this. They stand as models and inspiration for us all.

I hope you've enjoyed reading and learning about our work in *The Missing Piece* and want to take what you learned even further. If you are looking for more, check out our other products and take advantage of the free online Profile Assessment at RhysMethod.com. Or, to find out more about the Rhys Thomas Institute of Energy medicine, go to RhysThomasInstitute.com.

ABOUT THE AUTHOR

Rhys Thomas

Rhys Thomas is a visionary author, speaker and trainer in the energy medicine field. He is celebrated worldwide as a pioneer in energy medicine due to his synthesis and re-interpretation of energy medicine techniques for personal and professional transformation. He is the creator of the Rhys Method® transformational system taught exclusively at the Rhys Thomas Institute of Energy Medicine, and as part of Rhys Thomas Coaching Programs.

When he was 38, Rhys had an awakening experience that ended his struggle in life to be who he was truly born to be, not who he was supposed to be. He was introduced to what turned out to be "the missing piece," a powerful form of energy medicine that profoundly changed his life. From his awakening, Rhys could see that he was not alone. He discovered that the source of people's pain was trying to be someone they are supposed to be and not truly knowing who they are. With this realization, Rhys developed an easy to understand system of self-understanding that moves far beyond any other current systems, now called the Rhys Method Life Purpose Profile System®.

Today, Rhys has impacted tens of thousands of people through his videos, speaking events and programs, and through his Institute. He discovered that most people are looking for three basic things in life: Financial freedom in a career they are proud of, better relationships both personally and in business, and better health so they can enjoy their lives. He shows people how to find

Getting Clear About Your Soul's Purpose for Success in Life

what they want in three easy steps, which are to 1) get clear on your purpose and direction, 2) develop the habit of courage, and 3) raise your energy to follow your calling fearlessly.

Rhys is a graduate and former teacher at the Institute of Healing Arts and Sciences and the founder of The Rhys Thomas Institute of Energy Medicine and Solstice Healing Arts Center. He has 15 years of experience in energy medicine practice, which includes full spectrum healing, crystal bowl sound healing, energy reading, and soul reading. He is a certified Energy Medicine Practitioner, Reiki Master, and 2nd Degree Black Belt with 25 years of martial arts training. Before entering the healing arts, he had a successful 27-year career as a tennis professional and national speaker for the tennis industry.

Learn more and connect with Rhys at:
www.RhysMethod.com
www.RhysThomasInstitute.com